THE SENTIMENTAL BLOKE
AND OTHER VERSES

THE SENTIMENTAL BLOKE
AND OTHER VERSES

by

C. J. DENNIS

Chosen and Introduced
by
ALEC H. CHISHOLM

AUTHOR OF
The Making of a Sentimental Bloke

THE COLLECTOR'S LIBRARY OF
AUSTRALIA'S GREAT BOOKS

Published by
TIMES HOUSE

TIMES HOUSE PUBLISHING
61-69 Anzac Parade, Kensington, NSW 2033
Published by arrangement with
Angus & Robertson Publishers

First published by Angus & Robertson Publishers, Australia, 1915
Arkon edition 1976
Reprinted 1980
This Australia's Great Books edition, 1984
Reprinted 1986, 1987
© Angus & Robertson Publishers
ISBN 0 85835 694 5

Printed in Singapore
by Toppan Printing Co.

INTRODUCTION

Was there ever an autobiography, in fact or fiction, prose or verse, that opened in more forthright fashion than does the tale of Australia's Sentimental Bloke, as presented by C. J. Dennis:

> The world 'as got me snouted jist a treat;
>   Crool Forchin's dirty left 'as smote me soul;
> An' all them joys o' life I 'eld so sweet
>   Is up the pole!

The Bloke—known also as the Kid and Bill—was obviously at odds with the whole universe when he made that poignant complaint. But, of course, his condition was no novelty. Many a man before him had developed a fervent grouch against the world at large. Similar feelings had been expressed, for example, by another "Bill" of a much earlier day—one surnamed Shakespeare:

> When in disgrace with fortune and men's eyes
> I all alone beweep my outcast state,
> And trouble deaf heaven with my bootless cries,
> And look upon myself, and curse my fate.

If the language of the Shakespearian sonnet is rather more chaste than that of the Dennis song, the two expressions are impressively alike in substance. (They bear in fact the same relationship as do Hamlet's claim, "There's a divinity that shapes our ends", and the Bloke's crisp remark, "It's 'ow Gawd builds a bloke".) They are, moreover, alike in having a flavour of factual autobiography. That is to say, Dennis himself was in trouble with "Forchin's dirty left" just as often as Shakespeare was "in disgrace with fortune and men's eyes", and, no doubt, he found relief at times, as Shakespeare apparently did, in causing his spirit to "rail on Lady Fortune in good terms"—if only to prove that the clouds were usually followed by sunshine.

The career of C. J. Dennis was in fact quite extraordinary, even fantastic, in its varying facets. Necessarily, then, it needs to be considered, at least in outline, when the man's work is being assessed; and in presenting such an outline we may, with mild apologies, take the Shakespeare parallel just a little further. How remarkable it was, in the major case, that a youth from quiet Stratford-on-Avon became in time a profound student of life at Court, a skilled poetic weaver in many shades of language, and the greatest of all limners of the tempestuous drama of humanity! And how remarkable it was, in the minor case, that a youth from an Australian village, whose work during many years made no impression, leaped from obscurity in middle age, through the medium of one small book of verse, and attained national fame as Australia's Laureate of the Larrikin!

Clarence Michael James Dennis was born at Auburn, a village in the lower north of South Australia, on 7th September 1876. His father, James Dennis, a former master mariner, of Irish birth or extraction, had arrived in Auburn in the early eighteen-sixties and become licensee of an inn. He lost two children in infancy and his wife died soon afterwards (1874). Little more than a year later, at the age of 47, he married Catherine (Kate) Tobin, aged 24, member of an Irish family in the district that contained five daughters and one son. C. J. Dennis was the eldest of three sons of this union.

When the boy Clarrie was about seven years of age the family moved to Gladstone, fifty miles northward, and a few years later another transfer was made to a hotel at Laura, seven miles farther north again. Some of the boy's early schooling was gained at Gladstone, but most, it would appear, was acquired under the eyes of his four maiden aunts at the village of Mintaro. Prim and pious little women, those aunts seem to have believed their duty to lie in developing a rural edition of Little Lord Fauntleroy. They dressed the boy in a starchy suit, with Eton collar, peaked cap, and patent leather shoes, rounded off with brown gloves and a cane, and they trained him to raise that cap to every woman about the place. Consequently, the unfortunate "Clarence" became a favourite target for ribald lads of the village and so was forced to play mainly with girls.

Those experiences, in the case of a sensitive lad, may well have been soul-searing. And, by the same token, they may explain in some degree why Dennis later discarded the stately name of "Clarence" in favour of "Den", why he became at times quite unsocial, and why he made his chief literary occupation the production of "tough guys". Ginger Mick and the Bloke were well suited, no doubt, by Spadger's Lane and other dingy parts of Melbourne, but they appear to have had their origins, their "ancestry" as it were, in a quiet village in South Australia!

Kate Dennis died in 1890—in the same month, August, and at the same age, 39, as had the first Mrs Dennis. Loss of their mother was a heavy blow to Clarrie, scarcely 14, and the two younger boys, for the father, then aged 62, could not well control three young sons while coping with the trials of inn-keeping in a frontier town. The emergency was met by two of the faithful aunts; they removed from little Mintaro to a much less congenial spot, the Beetaloo Hotel at Laura, and there they did their best, if not always successfully, to guide their three nephews in the paths of dignity and piety.

Imagine, if possible, what those worthy little women—"Pansy" and "Buttercup" to Laura people—would have said if they could have foreseen certain startling developments that were to arise, partly perhaps through their own fond ministrations. Imagine their feelings had it been revealed that their eldest nephew, their cherished Clarence, had even then developed a furtive admiration for larrikins, and that in later years he would capture a continent with books of verse containing lines such as these:

> Me, that 'as done me stretch fer stoushin' Johns,
>   An' spen's me leisure gettin' on the shick,
> An' 'arf me nights down there, in Little Lons.,
>   Wiv Ginger Mick,
> Jist 'eadin' 'em, an' doin' in me gilt.
> Tough luck! I s'pose it's 'ow a man is built!

As C. J. Dennis grew to adulthood he shook off, outwardly at least, the inhibitions of earlier days. He became, indeed, something of a man-about-town in little Laura. He developed a fondness for cricket, a tendency to declaim to the girls about the need for reforming the world, and a marked taste for producing stage quips and for playing parts in light opera. Also, and rather more significantly, he acquired in odd moments a useful acquaintance with good verse and prose and revealed something of his own gift for rhyme in skits on local men and events.

Den's first occupation, aside from assisting his father, was as a junior clerk in the office of a Laura solicitor. Experience in Adelaide subsequently included a term on the staff of the *Critic*, a sedate little social weekly. Before reaching 21 he was back in the hotel at Laura. Local reports agree that he was not meant by Nature to be a barman. His father shared that view. Consequently, at the age of 22 or 23 the ex-clerk, ex-journalist, ex-barman found himself upon the road, bound for Broken Hill. He arrived in the isolated mining centre in a forlorn condition, wearing clothes that were virtually shreds and patches, plus tattered canvas shoes, and having a working capital of precisely one shilling and ninepence.

For several months then he struggled through a variety of profitless occupations, every one of which was too strenuous for a man of his modest physique. He used to say later that the experience nearly killed him; but in general he preferred not to talk of that chaotic portion of his career.

Early in the present century the wanderer found his way back to Adelaide and rejoined the staff of the *Critic*. This time he stayed longer—long enough to become editor of the little journal. Then, late in 1905, he joined several others—notably a lad named A. E. Martin, later a well-known novelist—in launching the *Gadfly*, a weekly journal devoted to cheerfully malicious comment on the Australian scene, and in particular to light satirical verse by its editor, C. J. Dennis.

When, after a couple of years, the wings of the *Gadfly* began to wilt through heavy financial weather, Dennis handed over to Martin and wandered away to Melbourne. Here he eked out an existence as a freelance journalist and in any other way that became available. With the possible exception of the period spent at Broken Hill, this appears to have been the most drab period of his life. He worked as well as may be, but he expended his slight funds and slight physique much too carelessly, and soon his appearance fell far below the dapper standard of *Gadfly* days.

He was rescued by an artist, Hal Waugh, who carried him off to a camp he had established at Toolangi, a picturesque highland settlement some forty miles east of Melbourne.

By this time, at the age of 31, Dennis had lived in five settlements and three cities, and never more than a few years at most in each. He himself would have been astonished, no doubt, if he could have foreseen that the latest place of residence was to be his home, more or less continuously, from 1908 until his death thirty years later.

At the beginning of his Toolangi citizenship he lived in Hal Waugh's tent. Later his gaze fell upon a small weatherboard house, formerly the home of a timberman; and as no one seemed either to own or to want the place he moved his few possessions into it and set himself up as a householder. There, of course, he continued to be his own cook, launderer, pants-patcher, and general house-keeper; and he supported himself by writing verse for various journals.

It was a lonely life. As the months and the years rolled on the one-time well-dressed editor came "mighty near to vegetating" and had to "work like blazes to fend off the blues". He was, indeed, experiencing personally the plight of the "bloke" whom he brought into being in this period, the fellow who complained of the impact of "Forchin's dirty left", and who declared roundly:

> I'm crook; me name is Mud; I've done me dash;
> Me flamin' spirit's got the flamin' 'ump!

Relief came in 1913. In that year R. H. Croll, an officer of the Victorian Education Department, who had chanced to drop in upon Dennis during a walking tour, introduced him to John Gari-baldi Roberts, a genial, book-loving official of the Melbourne Tramways Company. In that year, too, Dennis got together a selection from the verses he had published in various journals and had it issued in book form, by E. W. Cole of Melbourne, under the title of *Backblock Ballads and Other Verses*.

Roberts was impressed by Dennis's work. So were the men and women of art and letters who gathered about him, at week-ends, at his hospitable home, "Sunnyside", set among the hills at South Sassafras (now Kallista), some twenty-five miles east of Melbourne. The Sunnyside company appreciated in particular a challenging oddity that its author had termed "A Real Australian Austra—laise", and which had first appeared in November of 1908 as the winner of a special prize in a competition conducted by the Sydney *Bulletin* for a National Song.

Most of all, though, the "Sunnysiders" were attracted to the book by four sets of verses bearing the generic title, "The Senti-mental Bloke", together with an extensive glossary designed for the guidance of "the Thoroughly Genteel". The humour, the sentiment, the decorative language, and the rhyming dexterity manifest in these verses went to the making of a joyous novelty, and it was received with acclaim in many another spot besides Sassafras. Indeed, Dennis himself realized that he had hit upon something with distinct possibilities in the Bloke sequence, and even before meeting Roberts and the others (October 1913) he had produced several additional instalments of the quaint verse-tales.

The fact that *Backblock Ballads and Other Verses* met with only modest success did not matter very much. The important thing for Dennis was that his newly-found friends stimulated a mentality that was in danger of becoming sluggish, together with the fact that Roberts and his wife, both essentially warm-hearted, gave him a home at Sunnyside and made him a financial allowance conditional upon a certain amount of work being produced each week. Garry Roberts and his wife and their friends were, indeed, a decisive influence in the life of C. J. Dennis.

Nevertheless, after fluctuating for a few months between his shack at Toolangi and a home in an old tramcar at Sunnyside, Dennis suddenly conceived the idea of going off to Sydney. That was about the middle of 1914. His spirits then were so low that he felt, so he said, "just like flat soda-water", and he surmised the condition to be due to his "poor old abused system fretting for a little drug-produced excitement". Inevitably, therefore, while working for a few weeks in Sydney on a union journal he strayed from the straight path frequently, so that when he returned to Melbourne in August he had to be nursed at the Roberts suburban home and then sent to Sunnyside to recuperate.

Who was to suppose that within a year this frayed little wanderer, battered by hard adventure in bush and city of various States, would hold first place among Australian writers in public esteem?

Most of the Sentimental Bloke series had been written at Toolangi before the end of 1913, but its author's intention to try to have it published in book form was suspended while the later verses were running through the *Bulletin*. Moreover, when he did seek a publisher in 1914 it was only to meet with a prompt rejection from a Melbourne firm—which thus provided Australia's most eloquent example of a publisher's indiscretion. Trying again in March of 1915, Dennis wrote to Angus and Robertson of Sydney, enclosing the manuscript and suggesting that a subscription edition be published at five shillings a copy and a cheaper edition at a shilling. He was "pretty confident", he said, that he could get about three hundred subscribers for the five-shilling edition, and he offered to pay for circulars advertising the project!

Brushing aside Den's ideas about methods of publication, Angus and Robertson issued the book on the basis of their own judgment —with an introduction by Henry Lawson and illustrations by Hal Gye—and within three months of publication two editions, numbering rather more than 7000 copies, had been sold. Within the next three months *The Bloke* was in a fifth edition and sales were still sound. Later Dennis was given the information that 66,148 copies had been sold in rather less than eighteen months, that is, between the first date of publication, 16th October 1915, and 31st March 1917. The figure related only to Australia and New Zealand and did not include editions published in Britain, Canada, and the United States.

Obviously there was fairly sound reason for a somewhat bewildered author to readjust his earlier ambition—the quaint idea that it might be possible to sell three hundred copies! Here, in fact, was the most remarkable success-story in the history of Australian authorship, and its central figure was a middle-aged man who, beginning life as a molly-coddled country boy, and being himself only of slight physique, had risen suddenly from penury to affluence through the medium of city "he-men" born of his own imagination.

Nor did the success of the little book end there. It became in 1916 the subject of professional recitals in various cities, and later its story was both filmed and dramatized. It aroused, too, appreciation from men of literary eminence as well as the general public. H. G. Wells, E. V. Lucas, and W. J. Locke joined in the applause. So did parliaments and pulpits. A parson in Canada declared the book to be "fragrant with spiritual truths from the Hills of God".

If the transformed author was somewhat staggered by all this— if he marvelled at what the fairies had done for him, a fate-buffeted man of forty years, through the medium of one small book of verse—he did not allow either his creative or practical impulses to be subdued. Realizing that the emotions of wartime may have been a factor in the success of the book, he isolated one of the Bloke's cobbers, Ginger Mick, sent him "off to the flamin' war to stoush the foe", and followed his career along to his death at Gallipoli. Again using robust vernacular, he told the tale with salty humour and the same remarkable rhyming skill that animated *The Bloke*, and again, almost inevitably, the public response was prompt and thorough. In less than six months—to 31st March 1917—sales in Australia and New Zealand alone had reached the healthy total of 42,349 copies. The authentic flavour of the story was established by the cordial reception it received from men on active service, to whom it was introduced by a "pocket edition for the trenches".

Now the chequered career of C. J. Dennis had reached its climax. He could scarcely be expected to go on repeating the striking successes of *The Bloke* and *Ginger Mick*. Nor, on the other hand, was it at all likely that he would ever again be in need of succour— ever again find himself, as the Bloke had it:

> Jist moochin' round like some pore, barmy coot,
> Uv 'ope, an' joy, an' forchin destichoot.

The only question was, Would he be able to keep his head in the altered circumstances? None of Den's associates was at all sure how that question would be answered. Each of them had always found him to be an unpredictable little fellow. He was, they knew, fraternal enough at times, able and willing to play a part, sing, use a musical instrument, produce clever quips in prose or verse, and, with quite unpoetlike skill, manufacture almost anything from a banjo to a billiard-table. But they knew, too, that the Touchstone was apt at other times to turn into a Jaques—that he had a strong strain of reserve, amounting almost to shyness, could be cold to the point of arrogance for no particular reason, and in general was much less sentimental than his own Sentimental Bloke. Also, coupled with the physical contrast between the man himself and the "tough guys" of his imagination, there was the fact that, unlike his chief characters, he had little knowledge of the arts of " 'eadin' browns" (at two-up) and "chuckin' off chiack" (at girls); the sole indulgence he discussed from personal experience was what the Bloke described as "pourin' snake-juice in yer face", and the curious thing was that in all such outbreaks he was usually quite unsocial.

How, then, was anyone to predict with assurance what the future held for this man of contrasts who had sprung suddenly from obscurity to fame?

In 1915 Dennis had obtained somehow a job in the Commonwealth Public Service, but he gave that up in the following year and proceeded to become, like his own regenerated Bloke, an Established Citizen. He built a charming home, complete with garden, on the site of the old shack at Toolangi, got himself married in 1917 (to Olive, daughter of John Herron of Melbourne), and settled down to the production of a steady stream of books. The new house, "Arden", was his first real home: practically all of his earlier years had been spent in hotels (one had been his birthplace), in city lodgings, and in bush camps.

Six books and a booklet were issued during the first seven years spent at Arden. Most were sequels of The Bloke and Ginger Mick themes, but none attained the success of the parental volumes. The odd thing was the relative failure of the two non-vernacular books, *The Glugs of Gosh*, an extremely clever and diverting satire, and *A Book for Kids* (later re-issued with the title changed to *Roundabout*), a thoroughly engaging volume of verse and prose for youth. Both Dennis and his publisher were disappointed by the lukewarm attitude of the public to these books.

Possibly, however, there was some balm for the poet in the assurance given him publicly by the Lord Mayor of Sydney—the city in which he had been a derelict a few years previously—that he stood on the same plane of popularity with Australians as did Robert Burns with Scottish people the world over. (Had the Lord Mayor, one wonders, been setting "Scots Wha Hae" alongside "Fellers of Australier, blokes an' coves an' coots"?)

In 1922 Dennis became associated with the Melbourne *Herald*, and for that paper he poured out, during sixteen years, a spate of topical and semi-topical verse. The product of an extraordinarily facile mind, much of this verse was very diverting and all was shot through with verbal dexterity. It included a number of Rain Songs (for Dennis always remembered the blessing of rain in the "strange, shadeless land" of his youth); it included many clever parodies, and it included as well a number of the patriotic poems that caused their author to be regarded as a kind of unofficial Australian laureate. On at least thirty occasions he engaged in the melodious trumpeting of national observances such as Anzac Day and Armistice Day, and sometimes he brought the Sentimental Bloke to his aid in the tasks.

It may be added that at one stage, when Osbert Sitwell in England was charging 100 guineas each for "poem-portraits", the nimble-witted Dennis conceived the bright idea of executing "verse-photos", or "jingle-snapshots", on the mass-production principle. "The writer," he declared solemnly, "is prepared to supply these at 2/3 a dozen. Special marked-down price during our Winter Sale, 1/11½." After which he proceeded to submit samples of the "jingle-snapshots", beginning with a flapper and a politician, extending to various other oddities, and ending with an electric tram.

A considerable body of prose, too, was contributed by Dennis to the *Herald* during this period. It included "Epistles to Ab" (letters from a farmer to his son in the city), and a fantastic sequence, with almost every word mis-spelled, purporting to be written by Ben Bowyang of Gunn's Gully, a "character" who, with his friend and foil Bill Smith, has since become the subject of a popular comic strip. Although amusing enough, and interesting when given a flavour of autobiography, the prose generally was not distinguished. The verse, however—as may be gathered from quotations cited in the present writer's biography of Dennis—was often distinctly impressive, and doubtless a judicious selection of it would make a very agreeable book.

One of the various verse-series published in the *Herald* was, in fact, announced for publication in book form in 1927. Entitled "Just Miss Mix: the Chronicles of a Little Town", it rendered in rhyme, with characteristic humour and pathos, the reflections and the gossip of a country seamstress, and incidentally introduced many types familiar in every Australian country town. Oddly, however, the projected book did not emerge—and that in spite of the fact that Percy Leason, a skilled sketcher of rural "characters", had been engaged as illustrator.

Another enterprise that fell by the wayside was a series bearing the tentative title, "The Bloke Shakespeare", apparently an elaboration of the general scheme of the verses describing Bill and Doreen at "The Play". In this instance, perhaps, the reason of the failure was that Den had fallen from grace again. "My head is in the dust and my hand as I write trembles with guilty shame," he confessed to his publisher. He added, however, that his work as a book-producer had been chiefly affected by his "very unwise excursion into daily journalism", and possibly there was some substance to that claim. The extraordinary thing, indeed, is that he was able to achieve so much worthy verse while working against the clock each day—and it is not surprising that his work sometimes had to be done by other staff-men.

After 1924, therefore, only one volume, apart from the revised *Book for Kids*, was produced for Dennis. Published in 1935 under the title of *The Singing Garden*, it was a compilation of prose and short poems, mainly about birds, that had appeared in the *Herald*, and it was illustrated with some few decorations and a photograph of Arden. A photographic illustration in a Dennis book was a novelty, for although every one of the nine earlier works had been illustrated—a notable distinction for a writer of verse—in each instance the illustrator had been an artist—first David Low, then Hal Gye, and then (in the juvenile book) Dennis himself.

The curtain fell on 22nd June 1938. Dennis was then in the sixty-second year of his colourful life. He was buried in the suburban cemetery of Box Hill, and upon the tombstone were inscribed two lines from the last poem in his last book:

> Now is the healing, quiet hour that fills
> This gay, green world with peace and grateful rest.

"C. J. Dennis was the Robert Burns of Australia," said the Prime Minister of the day, J. A. Lyons, in a public tribute. "His work is animated by truth, simplicity, and very genuine feeling," said E. V. Lucas. And John Masefield, who in 1935 had paid Dennis a visit at Toolangi, declared that "poetry with such a universal appeal, reaching all classes of readers, must have great merits".

Apparently many people shared those views, for soon after the death of Dennis memorial groups in his honour were formed in both Melbourne and Sydney (the Sydney body set up a "C. J. Dennis Memorial Prize" for literature) and, later, residents of certain Victorian rural areas where the poet had lived also began to establish memorials—including a public hall. There was, too, a proposal to erect a commemorative plaque on the village hotel in South Australia that served him as a birthplace.

Obviously, the little rhymer of Toolangi and Kallista, who had been poor and practically unknown until nearly forty years of age, had made himself in his later years a distinctive figure in the literary history of Australia.

For all that, however, the enduring nature of Dennis's work still remains to be determined. Much of it, being born of World War I, was to some extent topical. Much of it, too, was rendered in language that may now have become somewhat out-moded. But, of course, other factors have to be considered. Discussing this subject in *Australian Literature* (1940) Morris Miller said it was probable that verse in the vernacular found the limit of its attraction sooner than verse in the traditional form, but, he added, the Sentimental Bloke and Doreen seemed likely to live "as long as ballad-poetry has a hold on the literature of Australia". Similarly, an American anthologist, David McCord, wrote as recently as 1945 that in spite of its slang (which, he said, could be "taken in through the pores"), *The Sentimental Bloke* should be published again in the United States. "I am convinced," he added, "that the book has more of the eternal values, not to mention humour, than most of the protein-fed or intellectualised literature about which the critics are shouting every day."

Now, with the appearance of a collected edition, the opportunity is available for the public generally to determine the merits of Dennis's work from a modern point of view. And, of course, judgment has to be made not only on the vernacular verse-tales but on that lilting fantasy *The Glugs of Gosh*, on the bush ballads, and on the merry and melodious verses for children that the versatile poet wrote.

Nine books, a booklet and a leaflet are represented here. Obviously, selecting had to be governed by the need to get the material into one volume of reasonable size. For that reason many worthy items have been omitted and cuts have been made here and there in the ones chosen. It is believed, however, that the material now presented is fairly representative of Dennis's work and that nothing of special significance has been overlooked.

In addition to the embarrassment caused by quantity, there has been difficulty in making a selection from the work because much of it is in connected story form. The poet himself encountered that difficulty when in 1929-30 he attempted to assemble material for a collected edition; and possibly it was the cause of his project not reaching fulfilment. In the present instance care has been taken to endeavour to maintain the sequence of all the verse-tales.

First place in the collection is given to an individual "song", the famous "Austra—laise", because it has several points of distinction. The first example of its author's work to become known in various countries, it won a special prize in a National Song Competition conducted by the Sydney *Bulletin* (1908), later appeared in Dennis's first book, and later again was issued as a leaflet for the use of Australia's soldiers in World War I. Possibly we may agree that its pungent verses are still significant—no less challenging now to "blokes an' coves an' coots" than they were when bawled forth by early Diggers on the march.

It can scarcely be expected, perhaps, that this book will be received, by a public that has changed in both personnel and nature since World War I, with the rapture that greeted the first appearance of *The Sentimental Bloke* and *Ginger Mick.* But, on the other hand, it seems highly probable that through the present medium many readers who are "getting along", including Old Diggers, will recapture some of the joys of yesteryear; and, in addition, it may reasonably be supposed that a newer generation will be blithely impressed by the humour, the sentiment, the extraordinary command of "slanguage", and the remarkable rhyming skill revealed by the former bush boy who became Australia's Laureate of the Larrikin.

ALEC H. CHISHOLM

Sydney, 1950

FOOTNOTE—RETROSPECTIVE

If one cannot fairly say "I told you so", there is justification, now, for claiming that the modified prediction made above has been fulfilled. The fact is, indeed, that the public of today has given this book a cordial welcome.

Whether its readers have been, and are, for the most part "new", or in the main those who enjoyed the verse-tales of Dennis when originally published, their demand has caused this volume to be reprinted so frequently, during merely a few years, that it is now in its sixth impression, making in all approximately 45,000 copies. This figure does not rival the high and rapid sales of *The Sentimental Bloke* and *Ginger Mick* in the days of World War I, but, when set against various circumstances, it is distinctly impressive. It indicates that, as John Masefield commented years ago, the verse of Dennis exercises a wide appeal, and, also, it suggests that Morris Miller was justified in predicting that the Bloke and Doreen are by way of being literary immortals.

These points are strengthened by the fact that although the greater part of *The Songs of a Sentimental Bloke* is given here, when that book was republished last year, as a complete unit, it too was accorded an appreciative reception. The welcome in both instances has been extended in other countries besides Australia. People elsewhere may be daunted by Australian slang as spoken, but they appear to "get by"

B

quite well when it appears in print, even if, occasionally, they have to consult a glossary. Possibly sight, rather than hearing, enables slang to be "taken in through the pores"!

It should be added that Dennis "revivals" of recent years have not been restricted to the present book and *The Sentimental Bloke*. Additionally, that challenging oddity "The Austra——laise" made yet another appearance, in 1951, when it was published as an adver-tisement, in many Australian newspapers, by the Commonwealth Director-General of Recruiting, the idea being that its "stirring national appeal" was as effective then "as ever before". Moreover in the following year—"Well, spare me bloomin' days!" as the Melbourne *Argus* exclaimed—the Bloke and Doreen made their bow in a ballet. Subsequent developments have included the erection of memorials to Dennis in his birthplace (Auburn, S.A.) and in the spot where he spent his later years (Toolangi, Vic.); the issuing of a book of remini-scences, *Down the Years*, by the poet's widow, and the publication of other reminiscences by two of Den's illustrators, Hal Gye and David Low.

Furthermore, other developments in Dennisiana are foreshadowed. Not content with having appeared in print, in recitals, in films, in a play, in songs, and in a ballet, the Bloke and Doreen are now, it is announced, to figure in a full-scale musical presentation of their story. In the near future, too, their creator is to meet the public again (posthumously) through the republication of *A Book for Kids*, a collection of merry verses (with illustrations) which was published in 1921 and re-issued, under the title *Roundabout*, in 1935.

Certain reviewers of the present volume (on its first appearance in 1950) are largely responsible for the decision to republish the *Book for Kids*, since, through having their youthful recollections stirred by extracts given here, they urged that the complete book, with its pic-turesque illustrations, should be made available to the youth of today.

Reviewers generally, it may fairly be added, gave a friendly greet-ing to the *Selected Verse of C. J. Dennis*, including the varied illustrations within and Broadhurst's "personality parade" on the dust-jacket. Some critics, it is true, were disposed to question Den's status as "the Laureate of the Larrikin", the suggestion of one being that there are really "very few pictures of larrikin-life" in the Bloke stories, and that of another being that the author leaned largely on *Jonah*, Louis Stone's novel of Sydney's byways published in 1911. These criticisms have substance. Dennis was not, in fact, an authority at firsthand on larrikinism, and, as I have said elsewhere, it is quite conceivable that he drew some of his inspiration from *Jonah*. Stone himself was quite certain on the point—and, rather oddly, he was not at all pleased by his brother-author's implied tribute.

Nevertheless, the general and particular appeal of Dennis's work remains unquestioned. A witness on this point is one of his early admirers, the Rev. F. W. Boreham (himself the author of many books). When reviewing the first edition of the present volume, in the *Australian Christian World*, Dr Boreham expressed again his appreciation of the "brilliance, human tenderness, and exuberant humour" manifested by the author of *The Sentimental Bloke* and other stories.

A.H.C.

Sydney, Feb.. 1958

CONTENTS

A REAL AUSTRALIAN
AUSTRA—LAISE

[This rousing "song" was the first of Dennis's writings to become widely known. Written in 1908 and entered as a joke in a National Song Competition conducted by the Sydney Bulletin, it was awarded a special prize, together with a tribute by the judge that it would "win its way to every heart in the backblocks". The Bulletin version contained only four verses. In 1913 the longer version appeared in Backblock Ballads and Other Verses, and in 1915 it was reprinted in leaflet form, as "A Marching Song, Dedicated to the A.I.F." The author recommended that it be sung to the tune of "Onward Christian Soldiers" and that "blessed", or "blooming", or any other suitable word be used to replace the dash. The fourth appearance of "The Austra—laise" was in Backblock Ballads and Later Verses (1918).]

THE AUSTRA—LAISE

FELLERS of Australier,
  Blokes an' coves an' coots,
Shift yer ——— carcases,
  Move yer ——— boots.
Gird yer ——— loins up,
  Get yer ——— gun,
Set the ——— enermy
  An' watch the ——— run.

CHORUS:

  Get a ——— move on,
    Have some ——— sense.
  Learn the ——— art of
    Self de- ——— -fence.

Have some ——— brains be-
  Neath yer ——— lids.
An' swing a ——— sabre
  Fer the missus an' the kids.
Chuck supportin' ——— posts,
  An' strikin' ——— lights,
Support a ——— fam'ly an'
  Strike fer yer ——— rights.

CHORUS:

  Get a ——— move, etc.

Joy is ——— fleetin',
  Life is ——— short.
Wot's the use uv wastin' it
  All on ——— sport?
Hitch yer ——— tip-dray
  To a ——— star.
Let yer ——— watchword be
  "Australi- ——— -ar!"

    Get a ——— move, etc.

'Ow's the ——— nation
  Goin' to ixpand
'Lest us ——— blokes an' coves
  Lend a ——— 'and?
'Eave yer ——— apathy
  Down a ——— chasm;
'Ump yer ——— burden with
  Enthusi- ——— -asm.

CHORUS:
    Get a ——— move, etc.

W'en the ——— trouble
  Hits yer native land
Take a ——— rifle
  In yer ——— 'and.
Keep yer ——— upper lip
  Stiff as stiff kin be,
An' speed a ——— bullet for
  Pos- ——— -terity.

CHORUS:
    Get a ——— move, etc.

W'en the ——— bugle
  Sounds "Ad- ——— -vance"
Don't be like a flock uv sheep
  In a ——— trance.
Biff the ——— foeman
  Where it don't agree.
Spifler- ——— -cate him
  To Eternity.

CHORUS:
    Get a ——— move, etc.

Fellers of Australier,
  Cobbers, chaps an' mates,
Hear the ——— enermy
  Kickin' at the gates!
Blow the ——— bugle,
  Beat the ——— drum,
Upper-cut and out the cow
  To kingdom- ——— -come!

CHORUS:
  Get a ——— move on,
    Have some ——— sense
  Learn the ——— art of
    Self de- ——— -fence!

THE SONGS OF A SENTIMENTAL BLOKE

[*The central character of this series of verse-tales—a city larrikin created in the bush!—first "dipped his lid" to the public through the columns of the* Bulletin *and through four "Songs" in the* Backblock Ballads *of 1913. Most of the material was written in a shack at Toolangi and the rest in an old tramcar, turned into a little home, at Kallista. When the complete "Bloke" book appeared (1915) with a preface by Henry Lawson and illustrations by Hal Gye, its success was immediate and record-breaking. In following years it reached several editions and was made the subject of recitals, a play, motion pictures, and broadcasts. Here nine of the fourteen songs are given.*

Lawson's preface, the only contribution of the kind to any of the Dennis books, opens with the suggestion that "a man can best write a preface to his own book, provided he knows it is good; also. if he knows it is bad". The Sentimental Bloke, Lawson says, "is more perfect than any alleged larrikin or Bottle-O character I ever attempted to sketch", and then he adds:

"The exquisite humour of *The Sentimental Bloke* speaks for itself; but there's a danger that its brilliance may obscure the rest, especially for minds, of all stations, that, apart from sport and racing, are totally devoted to boiling 'the cab-bitch stalks or somethink' in this social 'pickle found-ery' of ours.

"Doreen stands for all good women, whether down in the smothering alleys or up in the frozen heights.

"And so, having introduced the little woman (they all seem 'little' women), I 'dips me lid'— and stand aside."]

HAL GYE.

A SPRING SONG

THE world 'as got me snouted jist a treat;
  Crool Forchin's dirty left 'as smote me soul;
An' all them joys o' life I 'eld so sweet
  Is up the pole.
Fer, as the poit sez, me 'eart 'as got
The pip wiv yearnin' fer — I dunno wot.

I'm crook; me name is Mud; I've done me dash;
  Me flamin' spirit's got the flamin' 'ump!
I'm longin' to let loose on somethin' rash. . . .
  Aw, I'm a chump!
I know it; but this blimed ole Springtime craze
Fair outs me, on these dilly, silly days.

The young green leaves is shootin' on the trees,
  The air is like a long, cool swig o' beer,
The bonzer smell o' flow'rs is on the breeze,
  An' 'ere's me, 'ere,
Jist moochin' round like some pore, barmy coot,
Of 'ope, an' joy, an' forchin destichoot.

I've lorst me former joy in gittin' shick,
  Or 'eadin' browns; I 'aven't got the 'eart
To word a tom; an', square an' all, I'm sick
  Of that cheap tart
'Oo chucks 'er carkis at a feller's 'ead
An' mauls 'im . . . Ar! I wisht that I wus dead!

What *is* the matter wiv me? . . . I dunno.
  I got a sorter yearnin' 'ere inside,
A dead-crook sorter thing that won't let go
  Or be denied—
A feelin' like I want to do a break,
An' stoush creation for some woman's sake.

9

The little birds is chirpin' in the nest,
　The parks an' gardings is a bosker sight,
Where smilin' tarts walks up an' down, all dressed
　In clobber white.
An', as their snowy forms goes steppin' by,
It seems I'm seekin' somethin' on the sly:

Somethin' or someone—I don't rightly know;
　But, seems to me, I'm kind er lookin' for
A tart I knoo a 'undred years ago,
　Or, maybe, more.
Wot's this I've 'eard them call that thing? . . . Geewhizz
Me ideel bit o' skirt! That's wot it is!

Me ideel tart! . . . An', bli'me, look at me!
　Jist take a squiz at this, an' tell me can
Some square an' honist tom take this to be
　'Er own true man?
Aw, Gawd! I'd be as true to 'er, I would—
As straight an' stiddy as . . . Ar, wot's the good?

Me, that 'as done me stretch fer stoushin' Johns,
　An' spen's me leisure gittin' on the shick,
An' 'arf me nights down there, in Little Lons.,
　Wiv Ginger Mick,
Jist 'eadin' 'em, an' doin' in me gilt.
Tough luck! I s'pose it's 'ow a man is built.

It's 'ow Gawd builds a bloke; but don't it 'urt
　When 'e gits yearnin's fer this 'igher life,
On these Spring mornin's, watchin' some sweet skirt—
　Some fucher wife—
Go sailin' by, an' turnin' on his phiz
The glarssy eye—fer bein' wot 'e is.

I've watched 'em walkin' in the gardings 'ere—
　Cliners from orfices an' shops an' such;
The sorter skirts I dursn't come too near,
　Or dare to touch.
An' when I see the kind er looks they carst. . . .
Gorstrooth! Wot is the *use* o' me, I arst?

The little winds is stirrin' in the trees,
   Where little birds is chantin' lovers' lays;
The music of the sorft an' barmy breeze. . . .
   Aw, spare me days!
If this 'ere dilly feelin' doesn't stop
I'll lose me block an' stoush some flamin' cop!

C

THE INTRO

'Er name's Doreen . . . Well, spare me bloomin' days!
You could 'a' knocked me down wiv 'arf a brick!
   Yes, me, that kids meself I know their ways,
   An' 'as a name for smoogin' in our click!
I jist lines up an' tips the saucy wink.
But strike! The way she piled on dawg! Yer'd think
   A bloke was givin' back-chat to the Queen. . . .
     'Er name's Doreen.

I seen 'er in the markit first uv all,
Inspectin' brums at Steeny Isaacs' stall.
   I backs me barrer in—the same ole way—
   An' sez, "Wot O! It's been a bonzer day.
'Ow is it fer a walk?" . . . Oh, 'oly wars!
The sorter *look* she gimme! Jest becors
   I tried to chat 'er, like you'd make a start
     Wiv *any* tart.

An' I kin take me oaf I wus perlite,
An' never said no word that wasn't right,
   An' never tried to maul 'er, or to do
   A thing yeh might call crook. Ter tell yeh true,
I didn't seem to 'ave the nerve—wiv 'er.
I felt as if I couldn't go that fur,
   An' start to sling off chiack like I used.
     Not intrajuiced!

Nex' time I sighted 'er in Little Bourke,
Where she was in a job. I found 'er lurk
   Wus pastin' labels in a pickle joint,
   A game that—any'ow, that ain't the point.
Once more I tried ter chat 'er in the street,
But, bli'me! Did she turn me down a treat!
   The way she tossed 'er 'ead an' swished 'er skirt!
     Oh, it wus dirt!

A squarer tom, I swear, I never seen,
In all me natchril, than this 'ere Doreen.
    It wer'n't no guyver neither; fer I knoo
    That any other bloke 'ad Buckley's 'oo
Tried fer to pick 'er up. Yes, she wus square.
She jist sailed by an' lef' me standin' there
        Like any mug. Thinks I, "I'm out o' luck,"
            An' done a duck.

Well, I dunno. It's that way wiv a bloke.
If she'd ha' breasted up ter me an' spoke,
    I'd thort 'er jist a commin bit er fluff,
    An' then fergot about 'er, like enough.
It's jist like this. The tarts that's 'ard ter get
Makes you all 'ot to chase 'em, an' to let
        The cove called Cupid get an 'ammer-lock,
            An' lose yer block.

I know a bloke 'oo knows a bloke 'oo toils
In that same pickle found-ery. ('E boils
    The cabbitch storks or somethink.) Anyway,
    I gives me pal the orfis fer to say
'E 'as a sister in the trade 'oo's been
Out uv a job, an' wants ter meet Doreen;
        Then we kin get an intro, if we've luck.
            'E sez, "Ribuck."

O' course we worked the oricle; you bet!
But, struth, I ain't recovered frum it yet!
    'Twas on a Saturdee, in Colluns Street,
    An'—quite be accident, o' course—we meet.
Me pal 'e trots 'er up an' does the toff—
    'E allus wus a bloke fer showin' off.
        "This 'ere's Doreen," 'e sez. "This 'ere's the Kid."
            I dips me lid.

"This 'ere's Doreen," 'e sez. I sez "Good day."
An', bli'me, I 'ad nothin' more ter say!
    I couldn't speak a word, or meet 'er eye.
    Clean done me block! I never been so shy

Not since I wus a tiny little cub,
An' run the rabbit to the corner pub—
    Wot time the Summer days wus dry an' 'ot—
        Fer my ole pot.

I dunno 'ow I done it in the end.
I reckerlect I arst ter be 'er friend;
    An' tried ter play at 'andies in the park,
    A thing she wouldn't sight. Aw, it's a nark!
I gotter swear when I think wot a mug
I must 'a' seemed to 'er. But still I 'ug
    That promise that she give me fer the beach.
        The bonzer peach!

Now, as the poit sez, the days drag by
On ledding feet. I wish't they'd do a guy.
    I dunno 'ow I 'ad the nerve ter speak
    An' make that meet wiv 'er fer Sundee week!
But, strike! It's funny wot a bloke'll do
When 'e's all out . . . She's gorn, when I come-to.
    I'm yappin' to me cobber uv me mash. . . .
        I've done me dash!

'Er name's Doreen. . . . An' me—that thort I knoo
    The ways uv tarts, an' all that smoogin' game!
An' so I ort; fer ain't I known a few?
    Yet some'ow . . . I dunno. It ain't the same.
    I carn't tell *wot* it is; but, all I know,
I've dropped me bundle—an' I'm glad it's so.
    Fer when I come ter think uv wot I been. . . .
        'Er name's Doreen.

THE STOUSH O' DAY

Ar, these is 'appy days! An' 'ow they've flown—
　　Flown like the smoke of some inchanted fag;
Since dear Doreen, the sweetest tart I've known,
　　Passed me the jolt that made me sky the rag.
An' ev'ry golding day floats o'er a chap
　　Like a glad dream of some celeschil scrap.

Refreshed wiv sleep Day to the mornin' mill
　　Comes jauntily to out the nigger, Night.
Trained to the minute, confident in skill,
　　'E swaggers in the east, chock-full o' skite;
Then spars a bit, an' plugs Night on the point.
　　Out go the stars; an' Day 'as jumped the joint.

The sun looks up, an' wiv a cautious stare,
　　Like some crook keekin' o'er a winder sill
To make dead cert'in everythink is square,
　　'E shoves 'is boko o'er an Eastern 'ill,
Then rises, wiv 'is dial all a'grin,
　　An' sez, " 'Ooray! I knoo that we could win!"

Sure of 'is title then, the champeen Day
　　Begins to put on dawg among 'is push,
An', as he mooches on 'is gaudy way,
　　Drors tribute from each tree an' flow'r an' bush.
An', w'ile 'e swigs the dew in sylvan bars,
　　The sun shouts insults at the sneakin' stars.

Then, lo! the push o' Day rise to applaud;
　　An' all 'is creatures clamour at 'is feet
Until 'e thinks 'imself a little gawd,
　　An' swaggers on an' kids 'imself a treat.
The w'ile the lurkin' barrackers o' Night
　　Sneak in retreat an' plan another fight.

On thro' the hours, triumphant, proud an' fit,
   The champeen marches on 'is up'ard way,
Till, at the zenith, bli'me! 'e—is—IT!
   And all the world bows to the Boshter Day.
The jealous Night speeds messidges thro' space
   'Otly demandin' terms, an' time, an' place.

A w'ile the champeen scorns to make reply;
   'E's taken tickets on 'is own 'igh worth;
Puffed up wiv pride, an' livin' mighty 'igh,
   'E don't admit that Night is on the earth.
But as the hours creep on 'e deigns to state
   'E'll fight for all the earth an' 'arf the gate.

Late afternoon . . . Day feels 'is flabby arms,
   An' tells 'imself 'e don't seem quite the thing.
The 'omin' birds shriek clamorous alarms;
   An' Night creeps stealthily to gain the ring.
But see! The champeen backs an' fills, becos
   'E doesn't feel the Boshter Bloke 'e was.

Time does a bunk as us-u-al, nor stays
   A single instant, e'en at Day's be'est.
Alas, the 'eavy-weight's 'igh-livin' ways
   'As made 'im soft, an' large around the vest.
'E sez 'e's fat inside; 'e starts to whine;
   'E sez 'e wants to dror the color line.

Relentless nigger Night crawls thro' the ropes,
   Advancin' grimly on the quakin' Day,
Whose noisy push, shorn of their 'igh-noon 'opes,
   Wait, 'ushed an' anxious, fer the comin' fray.
And many lusty barrackers of noon
   Desert 'im one by one—traitors so soon!

'E's out er form! 'E 'asn't trained enough!
   They mark their sickly champeen on the stage,
An' narked, the sun, 'is backer, in a huff,
   Sneaks outer sight, red in the face wiv rage.
W'ile gloomy roosters, they 'oo made the morn
   Ring wiv 'is praises, creep to bed ferlorn.

All faint an' groggy grows the beaten Day;
  'E staggers drunkenly about the ring;
An owl 'oots jeerin'ly across the way,
  An' bats come out to mock the fallin' King.
Now, wiv a jolt, Night spreads 'im on the floor,
  An' all the west grows ruddy wiv 'is gore.

A single, vulgar star leers from the sky
  An' in derision, rudely mutters, "Yah!"
The moon, Night's conkerbine, comes glidin' by
  An' laughs a 'eartless, silvery "Ha-ha!"
Scorned, beaten, Day gives up the 'opeless fight,
  An' drops 'is bundle in the lap o' Night.

. . . .

So goes each day, like some celeschil mill,
  E'er since I met that shyin' little peach.
'Er bonzer voice! I 'ear its music still,
  As when she guv that promise fer the beach.
An', square an' all, no matter 'ow yeh start,
  The commin end of most of us is—Tart.

THE PLAY

"Wot's in a name?" she sez . . . And then she sighs,
An' clasps 'er little 'ands, an' rolls 'er eyes.
"A rose," she sez, "be any other name
Would smell the same.
Oh, w'erefore art you Romeo, young sir?
Chuck yer ole pot, an' change yer moniker!"

Doreen an' me, we bin to see a show—
The swell two-dollar touch. Bong tong, yeh know
A chair apiece wiv velvit on the seat;
A slap-up treat.
The drarmer's writ be Shakespeare, years ago,
About a barmy goat called Romeo.

"Lady, be yonder moon I swear!" sez 'e.
An then 'e climbs up on the balkiney;
An' there they smooge a treat, wiv pretty words,
Like two love-birds.
I nudge Doreen. She whispers, "Ain't it grand!"
'Er eyes is shinin'; an' I squeeze 'er 'and.

"Wot's in a name?" she sez. 'Struth, I dunno.
Billo is just as good as Romeo.
She may be Juli-er or Juli-et—
'E loves 'er yet.
If she's the tart 'e wants, then she's 'is queen,
Names never count . . . But ar, I like "Doreen!"

A sweeter, dearer sound I never 'eard;
Ther's music 'angs around that little word,
Doreen! . . . But wot was this I starts to say
About the play?
I'm off me beat. But when a bloke's in love
'Is thorts turn 'er way, like a 'omin' dove.

This Romeo 'e's lurkin' wiv a crew—
A dead tough crowd o' crooks—called Montague.
'Is cliner's push—wot's nicknamed Capulet—
They 'as 'em set.
Fair narks they are, jist like them back-street clicks.
Ixcep' they fights wiv skewers 'stid o' bricks.

Wot's in a name? Wot's in a string o' words?
They scraps in ole Verona wiv the'r swords,
An' never give a bloke a stray dog's chance,
An' that's Romance.
But when they deals it out wiv bricks an' boots
In Little Lon., they're low, degraded broots.

Wot's jist plain stoush wiv us, right 'ere to-day,
Is "valler" if yer fur enough away.
Some time, some writer bloke will do the trick
Wiv Ginger Mick,
Of Spadger's Lane. 'E'll be a Romeo,
When 'e's bin dead five 'undred years or so.

Fair Juli-et, she gives 'er boy the tip.
Sez she: "Don't sling that crowd o' mine no lip;
An' if you run agin a Capulet,
Jist do a get,"
'E swears 'e's done wiv lash; 'e'll chuck it clean.
(Same as I done when I first met Doreen.)

They smooge some more at that. Ar, strike me blue!
It gimme Joes to sit an' watch them two!
'E'd break away an' start to say good-bye,
An' then she'd sigh
"Ow, Ro-me-o!" an' git a strangle-holt,
An' 'ang around 'im like she feared 'e'd bolt.

Nex' day 'e words a gorspil cove about
A secrit weddin'; an' they plan it out.
'E spouts a piece about 'ow 'e's bewitched:
Then they git 'itched . . .
Now, 'ere's the place where I fair git the pip:
She's 'is for keeps, an' yet 'e lets 'er slip!

19

Ar! but 'e makes me sick! A fair gazob!
'E's jist the glarsey on the soulful sob,
'E'll sigh and spruik, an' 'owl a love-sick vow—
(The silly cow!)
But when 'e's got 'er, spliced an' on the straight,
'E crools the pitch, an' tries to kid it's Fate.

Aw! Fate me foot! Instid of slopin' soon
As 'e was wed, off on 'is 'oneymoon,
'Im an' 'is cobber, called Mick Curio,
They 'ave to go
An' mix it wiv that push o' Capulets.
They look fer trouble; an' it's wot they gets.

A tug named Tyball (cousin to the skirt)
Sprags 'em an' makes a start to sling off dirt.
Nex' minnit there's a reel ole ding-dong go—
'Arf round or so.
Mick Curio, 'e gets it in the neck,
"Ar, rats!" 'e sez, an' passes in 'is check.

Quite natchril, Romeo gits wet as 'ell.
"It's me or you!" 'e 'owls, an' wiv a yell,
Plunks Tyball through the gizzard wiv 'is sword,
'Ow I ongcored!
"Put in the boot!" I sez. "Put in the boot!"
"Ush!" sez Doreen . . . "Shame!" sez some silly coot

Then Romeo, 'e dunno wot to do.
The cops gits busy, like they allwiz do,
An' nose around until 'e gits blue funk
An' does a bunk.
They wants 'is tart to wed some other guy.
"Ah, strike!" she sez. "I wish that I could die!"

Now, this 'ere gorspil bloke's a fair shrewd 'ead.
Sez 'e, "I'll dope yeh, so they'll *think* yer dead."
(I tips 'e was a cunnin' sort, wot knoo
A thing or two).
She takes 'is knock-out drops, up in 'er room:
They think she's snuffed, an' plant 'er in 'er tomb.

Then things gits mixed a treat an' starts to whirl.
'Ere's Romeo comes back an' finds 'is girl
Tucked in 'er little coffing, cold an' stiff,
An' in a jiff
'E swallers lysol, throws a fancy fit,
'Ead over turkey, an' 'is soul 'as flit.

Then Juli-et wakes up an' sees 'im there,
Turns on the water-works an' tears 'er 'air,
"Dear love," she sez, "I cannot live alone!"
An', wif a moan,
She grabs 'is pockit knife, an' ends 'er cares . . .
"Peanuts or lollies!" sez a boy upstairs.

MAR

" 'ER pore dear Par," she sez, " 'e kept a store;"
An' then she weeps an' stares 'ard at the floor.
 " 'Twas thro' 'is death," she sez, "we wus rejuiced
To this," she sez . . . An' then she weeps some more.

" 'Er Par," she sez, "me poor late 'usband, kept
An 'ay an' corn store. 'E'd no faults ixcept
 'Im fallin' 'eavy orf a load o' charf
W'ich—killed 'im—on the—" 'Struth! But 'ow she wept.

She blows 'er nose an' sniffs. " 'E would 'a' made,"
She sez, "a lot of money in the trade.
 But, 'im took orf so sudden-like, we found
'E 'adn't kept 'is life insurince paid.

"To think," she sez, "a child o' mine should be
Rejuiced to workin' in a factory!
 If 'er pore Par 'e 'adn't died," she sobs . . .
I sez, "It wus a bit o' luck for me."

Then I gits red as 'ell, "That is—I mean,"
I sez, "I mighter never met Doreen
 If 'e 'ad not"—an' 'ere I lose me block—
"I 'ope," I sez, " 'e snuffed it quick and clean."

An' that wus 'ow I made me first deboo.
I'd dodged it cunnin' fer a month or two.
 Doreen she sez, "You'll 'ave to meet my Mar
Some day," she sez. An' so I seen it thro'.

I'd pictered some stern female in a cap
Wot puts the fear o' Gawd into a chap.
 An' 'ere she wus, aweepin' in 'er tea
An' drippin' moistcher like a leaky tap.

Two dilly sorter dawgs made outer delf
Stares 'ard at me frum orf the mantleshelf;
   I seemed to symperthise wiv them there pups;
I felt so stiff an' brittle-like meself.

Clobber? Me trosso, 'ead to foot, wus noo—
Got up regardless, fer this interview:
   Stiff shirt, a Yankee soot split up the back,
A tie wiv yeller spots an' stripes o' blue.

Me cuffs kep' playin' wiv me nervis fears,
Me patent leathers nearly brought the tears.
   An' there I sits wiv, "Yes, mum. Thanks. Indeed?"
Me stand-up collar sorin' orf me ears.

"Life's 'ard," she sez, an' then she brightens up:
"Still, we 'ave alwus 'ad our bite and sup.
   Doreen's been *sich* a help; she 'as indeed.
Some more tea, Willy? 'Ave another cup."

Willy! O, 'ell! 'Ere wus a flamin' pill!
A moniker that alwus makes me ill.
   "If it's the same to you, mum," I replies,
"I answer quicker to the name of Bill."

Up goes 'er 'ands an' eyes, "That vulgar name!
No, Willy, but it isn't all the same;
   My fucher son must be respectable."
"Orright," I sez, "I s'pose it's in the game."

"Me fucher son," she sez, "right on frum this
Must not take anythink I say amiss.
   I know me jooty be me son-in-lor;
So, Willy, come an' give yer Mar a kiss."

I done it. Tho' I dunno 'ow I did.
"Dear boy," she sez, "to do as you are bid.
   Be kind to 'er," she sobs, "my little girl!"
An' then I kiss Doreen. Sez she, "Ah, Kid!"

Doreen! Ar 'ow 'er pretty eyes did shine.
No sight on earth or 'Eaven's 'arf so fine,
   An' as they looked at me she seemed to say
"I'm proud of 'im, I am, an' 'e is mine."

There wus a sorter glimmer in 'er eye,
An 'appy, nervis look, 'arf proud, 'arf shy;
   I seen 'er in me mind be'ind the cups
In our own little kipsie, bye an' bye.

An' then when Mar-in-lor an' me began
To tork of 'ouse'old things an' scheme an' plan,
   A sudden thort fair jolts me where I live:
"These is my wimmin folk! An' I'm a man!"

It's wot they calls responsibility.
All of a 'eap that feelin' come to me;
   An' somew'ere in me 'ead I seemed to feel
A sneakin' sort o' wish that I was free.

'Ere's me, 'oo never took no 'eed o' life,
Investin' in a mar-in-lor an' wife:
   Someone to battle fer besides meself,
Somethink to love an' shield frum care and strife.

" 'Er pore dead Par," she sez, an' gulps a sob.
An' then I tells 'er 'ow I got a job
   As storeman down at Jones' printin' joint,
A decent sorter cop at fifty bob.

Then things get 'ome-like; an' we torks till late,
An' tries to tease Doreen to fix the date,
   An' she gits suddin soft and tender-like,
An' cries a bit, when we parts at the gate.

An', as I'm moochin' 'omeward frum the car,
A suddin notion stops me wiv a jar—
   Wot if Doreen, I thinks, should grow to be
A fat ole weepin' willer like 'er Mar!

O, 'struth! It won't bear thinkin' of! It's crook!
An' I'm a mean, unfeelin' dawg to look
　　At things like that. Doreen's Doreen to me,
The sweetest peach on w'ich a man wus shook

'Er "pore dear Par" . . . I s'pose 'e 'ad 'is day,
An' kissed an' smooged an' loved 'er in 'is way.
　　An' wed an' took 'is chances like a man—
But, Gawd! this splicin' racket ain't all play.

Love is a gamble, an' there ain't no certs.
Some day, I s'pose, I'll git wise to the skirts,
　　An' learn to take the bitter wiv the sweet . . .
But, strike me purple! "Willie!" *That's* wot 'urts.

HITCHED

"An'—wilt—yeh—take—this—woman—fer—to be—
   Yer—weddid—wife?" . . . O, strike me! Will I wot?
Take 'er? Doreen? 'E stan's there *arstin'* me!
   As if 'e thort per'aps I'd rather not!
   Take 'er? 'E seemed to think 'er kind was got
Like cigarette-cards, fer the arstin'. Still,
   I does me stunt in this 'ere hitchin' rot,
An' speaks me piece: "Righto!" I sez, "I will."

"I will," I sez. An' tho' a joyful shout
   Come from me bustin' 'eart—I know it did—
Me voice got sorter mangled comin' out,
   An' makes me whisper like a frightened kid.
   "I will," I squeaks. An' I'd 'a' give a quid
To 'ad it on the quite, wivout this fuss,
   An' orl the starin' crowd that Mar 'ad bid
To see this solim hitchin' up of us.

"Fer—rich-er—er—fer—poor-er." So 'e bleats.
   "In—sick-ness—an'—in—'ealth." . . . An' there I stands,
An' dunno 'arf the chatter I repeats,
   Nor wot the 'ell to do wiv my two 'ands.
   But 'e don't 'urry puttin' on our brands—
This white-'aired pilot-bloke—but gives it lip,
   Dressed in 'is little shirt, wiv frills an' bands.
"In sick-ness—an'—in—" Ar! I got the pip!

An' once I missed me turn; an' Ginger Mick,
   'Oo's my best-man, 'e ups an' beefs it out.
   "I will!" 'e 'owls; an' fetches me a kick.
   "Your turn to chin!" 'e tips wiv a shout.
   An' there I'm standin' like a gawky lout.
(Aw, spare me! But I seemed to be *all* 'ands!)
   An' wonders wot 'e's goin' crook about,
Wiv 'arf a mind to crack 'im where 'e stands.

26

O, lumme! But ole Ginger was a trick!
  Got up regardless fer the solim rite
('E 'awks the bunnies when 'e toils, does Mick)
  An' twice I saw 'im feelin' fer a light
  To start a fag; an' trembles lest 'e might,
Thro' force o' habit like. 'E's nervis too;
  That's plain, fer orl 'is air o' bluff an' skite;
An' jist as keen as me to see it thro'.

But, 'struth, the wimmin! 'Ow they love this frill!
  Fer Auntie Liz, an' Mar, o' course, wus there;
An' Mar's two uncles' wives, an' Cousin Lil,
  An' 'arf a dozen more to grin and stare.
  I couldn't make me 'ands fit anywhere!
I felt like I wus up afore the Beak!
  But my Doreen she never turns a air,
Nor misses once when it's 'er turn to speak.

"To—be—yer—weddid—wife—" Aw, take a pull!
  Wot in the 'ell's 'e think I come there for?
An' so 'e drawls an' drones until I'm full,
  An' wants to do a duck clean out the door.
  An' yet, fer orl 'is 'igh-falutin' jor,
Ole Snowy wus a reel good-meanin' bloke;
  If 'twasn't fer the 'oly look 'e wore
Yeh'd think 'e piled it on jist fer a joke.

An', when at last 'e shuts 'is little book,
  I 'eaves a sigh that nearly bust me vest.
But, 'Eavens! Now 'ere's muvver goin' crook!
  An' sobbin' awful on me manly chest!
  (I wish sh'd give them water-works a rest.)
"My little girl!" she 'owls. "O, treat 'er well!
  She's young—too young to leave 'er muvver's nest!"
"Orright, ole chook," I nearly sez. O, 'ell!

An' then we 'as a beano up at Mar's—
  A slap-up feed, wiv wine an' two big geese.
Doreen sits next ter me, 'er eyes like stars.
  O, 'ow I wished their blessed yap would cease!

D

The Parson-bloke 'e speaks a little piece,
That makes me blush an' 'ang me sillly 'ead.
    'E sez 'e 'opes our lovin' will increase—
I *likes* that pilot fer the things 'e said.

'E sez Doreen an' me is in a boat,
    An' sailin' on the matrimonial sea;
'E sez as 'ow 'e 'opes we'll allus float
    In peace an' joy, from storm an' danger free.
    Then muvver gits to weepin' in 'er tea;
An' Auntie Liz sobs like a winded colt;
    An' Cousin Lil comes 'round an' kisses me;
Until I feel I'll 'ave to do a bolt.

Then Ginger gits end-up an' makes a speech—
    ('E'd 'ad a couple, but 'e wasn't shick).
"My cobber 'ere," 'e sez, "'as copped a peach!
    Of orl the barrer-load she is the pick!
    I 'opes 'e won't fergit 'is pals too quick
As wus 'is frien's in olden days, becors,
    I'm trustin', later on," sez Ginger Mick,
"To celebrate the chris'nin'." . . . 'Oly wars!

At last Doreen an' me we gits away,
    An' leaves 'em doin' nothin' to the scran.
(We're honey-moonin' down beside the Bay.)
    I gives a 'arf a dollar to the man
    Wot drives the cab; an' like two kids we ran
To ketch the train—Ah, strike! I could 'a' flown!
    We gets the carridge right agen the van.
She whistles, jolts, an' starts . . . An' we're alone!

Doreen an' me! My precious bit o' fluff!
    Me own true weddid wife! . . . An' we're alone!
She seems so frail, an' me so big an' rough—
    I dunno wot this feelin' is that's grown
    Inside me 'ere that makes me feel I own
A thing so tender like I fear to squeeze
    Too 'ard fer fear she'll break . . . Then, wiv a groan
I starts to 'ear a coot call, "Tickets, please!"

You could 'a' outed me right on the spot!
    I wus so rattled when that porter spoke;
Fer, 'struth! them tickets I 'ad fair forgot!
    But 'e jist laughs, an' takes it fer a joke.
    "We must ixcuse," 'e sez, "new-married folk."
An' I pays up, an' grins, an' blushes red . . .
    It shows 'ow married life improves a bloke:
If I'd bin single I'd 'a' punched 'is 'ead!

UNCLE JIM

"I got no time fer wasters, lad," sez 'e
   "Give me a man wiv grit," sez Uncle Jim.
'E bores 'is cute ole eyes right into me,
   While I stares 'ard an' gives it back to 'im.
Then orl at once 'e grips me 'and in 'is:
"Some'ow," 'e sez, "I likes yer ugly phiz."

"You got a look," 'e sez, "like you could stay;
   Altho' yeh mauls King's English when yeh yaps
An' 'angs flash frills on ev'rythink yeh say.
   I ain't no grammarist meself, per'aps,
But langwidge is a 'elp, I owns," sez Unk,
"When things is goin' crook." An' 'ere 'e wunk.

"Yeh'll find it tough," 'e sez, "to knuckle down.
   Good farmin' is a gift—like spoutin' slang.
Yeh'll 'ave to cut the luxuries o' town,
   An' chuck the manners of this back-street gang;
Fer country life ain't cigarettes and beer."
"I'm game," I sez. Sez Uncle, "Put it 'ere!"

Like that I took the plunge, an' slung the game.
   I've parted wiv them joys I 'eld most dear;
I've sent the leery bloke that bore me name
   Clean to the pack wivout one pearly tear;
An' frum the ashes of a ne'er-do-well
A bloomin' farmer's blossomin' like 'ell.

Farmer! That's me! Wiv this 'ere strong right 'and
   I've gripped the plough; and blistered jist a treat.
Doreen an' me 'as gone upon the land.
   Yours truly fer the burden an' the 'eat!
Yours truly fer upendin' chunks o' soil!
The 'ealthy, 'ardy, 'appy son o' toil!

I owns I've 'ankered fer me former joys;
    I've 'ad me hours o' broodin' on me woes;
I've missed the comp'ny, an' I've missed the noise,
    The football matches an' the picter shows.
I've missed—but, say, it makes me feel fair mean
To whip the cat; an' then see my Doreen.

To see the colour comin' in 'er cheeks,
    To see 'er eyes grow brighter day be day,
The new, glad way she looks an' laughs an' speaks
    Is worf ten times the things I've chucked away.
An' there's a secret, whispered in the dark,
'As made me 'eart sing like a flamin' lark.

Jist let me tell yeh 'ow it come about.
    The things that I've been thro' 'ud fill a book.
Right frum me birf Fate played to knock me out;
    The 'and that I 'ad dealt to me was crook!
Then comes Doreen, an' patches up me parst;
Now Forchin's come to bunk wiv me at larst.

First orf, one night poor Mar gits suddin fits,
    An' floats wivout the time to wave "good-byes".
Doreen is orl broke up the day she flits;
    It tears me 'eart in two the way she cries.
To see 'er grief, it almost made me glad
I never knowed the mar I must 'ave 'ad.

We done poor Muvver proud when she went out—
    A slap-up send-orf, trimmed wiv tears an' crape.
An' then fer weeks Doreen she mopes about,
    An' life takes on a gloomy sorter shape.
I watch 'er face git pale, 'er eyes grow dim;
Till—like some 'airy angel—comes ole Jim.

A cherub togged in sunburn an' a beard
    An' duds that shouted "'Ayseed!" fer a mile:
Care took the count the minute 'e appeared,
    An' sorrer shrivelled up before 'is smile,
'E got the 'ammer-lock on my good-will
The minute that 'e sez, "So, this is Bill."

It's got me beat. Doreen's late Par, some way,
  Was second cousin to 'is bruvver's wife.
Somethin' like that. In less than 'arf a day
  It seemed 'e'd been my uncle orl me life.
'E takes me 'and: "I dunno 'ow it is,"
'E sez, "but, lad, I likes that ugly phiz."

An' when 'e'd stayed wiv us a little while
  The 'ouse begun to look like 'ome once more.
Doreen she brightens up beneath 'is smile,
  An' 'ugs 'im till I kids I'm gettin' sore.
Then, late one night, 'e opens up 'is scheme,
An' passed me wot looks like some fond dream.

'E 'as a little fruit-farm, doin' well;
  'E saved a tidy bit to see 'im thro';
'E's gittin' old fer toil, an' wants a spell;
  An' 'ere's a 'ome jist waitin' fer us two.
"It's 'er's an' yours fer keeps when I am gone,"
Sez Uncle Jim. "Lad, will yeh take it on?"

So that's the strength of it. An' 'ere's me now
  A flamin' berry farmer, full o' toil;
Playin' joo-jitsoo wiv an 'orse an' plough,
  An' coaxin' fancy tucker frum the soil;
An' longin', while I wrestles with the rake,
Fer days when my poor back fergits to ache.

Me days an' nights is full of schemes an' plans
  To figger profits an' cut out the loss;
An when the pickin's on, I 'ave me 'an's
  To take me orders while I act the boss;
It's sorter sweet to 'ave the right to rouse . . .
An' my Doreen's the lady of the 'ouse.

To see 'er bustlin' 'round about the place,
  Full of the simple joy o' doin' things,
That thoughtful, 'appy look upon 'er face,
  That 'ope an' peace an' pride o' labour brings,
Is worth the crowd of joys I knoo one time,
An' makes regrettin' 'em seem like a crime.

An' ev'ry little while ole Uncle Jim
   Comes up to stay a bit an' pass a tip.
It gives us 'eart jist fer to look at 'im,
   An' feel the friendship in 'is warm 'and-grip.
'Im, wiv the sunburn on 'is kind ole dile;
  'Im, wiv the sunbeams in 'is sweet ole smile.

"I got no time fer wasters, lad," sez 'e,
   "But that there ugly mug o' yourn I trust."
An' so I reckon that it's up to me
   To make a bloomin' do of it or bust.
I got to take the back-ache wiv the rest,
An' plug along, an' do me little best.

Luck ain't no steady visitor, I know;
   But now an' then it calls—fer look at me!
You wouldn't take me, 'bout a year ago,
   Free gratis wiv a shillin' pound o' tea;
Then, in a blessed 'eap, ole Forchin lands
A missus an' a farm fair in me 'ands.

THE KID

My son! . . . Them words, jist like a blessed song,
Is singin' in me 'eart the 'ole day long;
   Over an' over; while I'm scared I'll wake
   Out of a dream, to find it all a fake.

My son! Two little words, that, yesterdee,
Wus jist two simple, senseless words to me;
   An' now—no man, not since the world begun,
   Made any better pray'r that . . . My son!

A little while ago it was jist "me"—
A lonely, longin' streak o' misery.
   An' then 'twas " 'er an' me"—Doreen, my wife!
   An' now it's " 'im an' us," an'—sich is life!

But, 'struth! 'E is king-pin! The 'ead serang!
I mustn't tramp about, or talk no slang;
   I mustn't pinch 'is nose, or make a face,
   I mustn't—Strike! 'E seems to own the place!

"Goog, goo," 'e sez, an' curls 'is cunnin' toes.
Yeh'd be su'prised the 'eaps o' things 'e knows.
   I'll swear 'e tumbles I'm 'is father, too;
   The way 'e squints at me, an' sez, "Goog, goo."

"Goog, goo," 'e sez. I'll swear yeh never did
In all yer natcheril see sich a kid.
   The cunnin' ways 'e's got; the knowin' stare—
   Ther' ain't a youngster like 'im *anywhere*!

An', when 'e gets a little pain inside,
'Is dead straight griffin ain't to be denied.
   I'm sent to talk sweet nuffin's to the fowls;
   While nurse turns 'and-springs ev'ry time 'e 'owls.

But, say, I tell yeh straight . . . I been thro' 'ell!
The things I thort I wouldn't dare to tell
   Lest, in the tellin' I might feel again
   One little part of all that fear an' pain.

It come so sudden that I lorst me block.
First, it was 'ell-fer-leather to the doc.,
   'Oo took it all so calm 'e made me curse—
   An' then I sprints like mad to get the nurse.

By gum; that woman! But she beat me flat!
A man's jist putty in a game like that.
   She owned me 'appy 'ome almost before
   She fairly got 'er nose inside me door.

I wus too weak wiv funk to start an' rouse.
'Struth! Ain't a man the boss in 'is own 'ouse?
   "You go an' chase yerself!" she tips me straight.
   "Ther's nothin' now fer you to do but—wait."

Wait? . . . Gawd! . . . I never knoo wot waitin' meant
In all me life, till that day I was sent
   To loaf around, while there inside—Aw, strike!
   I couldn't tell yeh wot that hour was like!

Three times I comes to listen at the door;
Three times I drags meself away once more;
   'Arf dead wiv fear; 'arf filled wiv tremblin' joy . . .
   An' then she beckons me, an' sez—"A boy!"

"A boy!" she sez. "An' bofe is doin' well!"
I drops into a chair, an' jist sez—"'Ell!"
   It was a pray'r. I feels bofe crook an' glad . . .
   An' that's the strength of bein' made a dad.

I thinks of church when in that room I goes,
'Oldin' me breaf an' walkin' on me toes;
   Fer 'arf a mo' I feared me nerve 'ud fail
   To see 'er lying there so still an' pale.

She looks so frail, at first, I dursn't stir.
An' then, I leans acrost an' kisses 'er;
　　An' all the room gits sorter blurred an' dim . . .
　　She smiles, an' moves 'er 'ead. "Dear lad! Kiss 'im."

Near smothered in a ton of snowy clothes,
First thing, I sees a bunch o' stubby toes,
　　Bald 'ead, termater face, an' two big eyes.
　　"Look, Kid," she smiles at me. "Ain't 'e a size?"

'E didn't seem no sorter size to me;
But yet, I speak no lie when I agree;
　　" 'E is," I sez, an' smiles back at Doreen,
　　"The biggest nipper fer 'is age I've seen."

She turns away; 'er eyes is brimmin' wet.
"Our little son!" she sez. "Our precious pet!"
　　An' then, I seen a great big drop roll down
　　An' fall—kersplosh!—fair on 'is nibs's crown.

An' still she smiles. "A lucky sign," she said.
"Somewhere, in some ole book, one time I read,
　　'The child will sure be blest all thro' the years
　　Who's christened wiv 'is mother's 'appy tears.'"

　　　　·　　·　　·　　·　　·　　·　　·

My wife an' fam'ly! Don't it sound all right!
That's wot I whispers to meself at night.
　　Some day, I s'pose, I'll learn to say it loud
　　An' careless—kiddin' that I don't feel proud.

My son! . . . If ther's a Gawd 'oo's leanin' near
To watch our dilly little lives down 'ere,
　　'E smiles, I guess, if 'E's a lovin' one—
　　Smiles, friendly-like, to 'ear them words—My son.

THE MOOCH O' LIFE

This ev'nin' I was sittin' wiv Doreen,
  Peaceful an' 'appy wiv the day's work done,
Watchin', be'ind the orchard's bonzer green,
  The flamin' wonder of the settin' sun.

Another day gone by; another night
Creepin' along to douse Day's golden light;
  Another dawnin', when the night is gone,
  To live an' love—an' so life mooches on.

Times I 'ave thought, when things was goin' crook,
  When 'Ope turned nark an' Love forgot to smile,
Of somethin' I once seen in some ole book
  Where an ole sore-'ead arsts, "Is life worf w'ile?"

But in that stillness, as the day grows dim,
An' I am sittin' there wiv 'er an' 'im—
  My wife, my son! an' strength in me to strive,
  I only know—it's good to be alive!

Yeh live, yeh love, yeh learn; an' when yeh come
  To square the ledger in some thortful hour,
The everlastin' answer to the sum
  Must allus be, "Where's sense in gittin' sour?"

Fer when yeh've come to weigh the good an' bad—
The gladness wiv the sadness you 'ave 'ad—
  Then 'im 'oo's faith in 'uman goodness fails
  Fergits to put 'is liver in the scales.

Livin' an' lovin'; learnin' day be day;
  Pausin' a minute in the barmy strife
To find that 'elpin' others on the way
  Is gold coined fer your profit—sich is life.

I've studied books wiv yearnin's to improve,
To 'eave meself out of me lowly groove,
   An' 'ere is orl the change I ever got:
   "'Ark at yer 'eart, an' you kin learn the lot."

I gives it in—that wisdom o' the mind—
   I wasn't built to play no lofty part.
Orl such is welkim to the joys they find;
   I only know the wisdom o' the 'eart.

An' ever it 'as taught me, day be day,
The one same lesson in the same ole way:
   "Look fer yer profits in the 'earts o' friends,
   Fer 'atin' never paid no dividends."

Life's wot yeh make it; an' the bloke 'oo tries
To grab the shinin' stars frum out the skies
   Goes crook on life, an' calls the world a cheat,
   An' tramples on the daisies at 'is feet.

But when the moon comes creepin' o'er the hill,
   An' when the mopoke calls along the creek,
I takes me cup o' joy an' drinks me fill,
   An' arsts meself wot better could I seek.

An' ev'ry song I 'ear the thrushes sing
That everlastin' message seems to bring;
   An' ev'ry wind that whispers in the trees
   Gives me the tip there ain't no joys like these.

Livin' an' lovin'; wand'rin' on yer way;
   Reapin' the 'arvest of a kind deed done;
An' watchin', in the sundown of yer day,
   Yerself again, grown nobler in yer son.

Knowin' that ev'ry coin o' kindness spent
Bears interest in yer 'eart at cent per cent;
   Measurin' wisdom by the peace it brings
   To simple minds that values simple things.

An' when I take a look along the way
  That I 'ave trod, it seems the man knows best,
Who's met wiv slabs of sorrer in 'is day,
  When 'e is truly rich an' truly blest.

An' I am rich, becos me eyes 'ave seen
The lovelight in the eyes of my Doreen;
  An' I am blest, becos me feet 'ave trod
  A land 'oo's fields reflect the smile o' God.

Livin' an' lovin'; learnin' to fergive
  The deeds an' words of some un'appy bloke
Who's missed the bus—so 'ave I come to live,
  An' take the 'ole mad world as 'arf a joke.

. . . .

Sittin' at ev'nin' in this sunset-land,
Wiv 'Er in all the World to 'old me 'and,
  A son, to bear me name when I am gone. . . .
  Livin' an' lovin'—so life mooches on.

THE MOODS OF GINGER MICK

[*A sequel to* The Sentimental Bloke, *the story
of Ginger Mick (1916) followed its predecessor
in achieving high success in Australia and New
Zealand, being published in America, and
attaining warm popularity with troops on service
through the medium of a Pocket Edition for the
Trenches. Fourteen poems appeared in the
volume; eight of them are given here.*]

HAL GYE .

WAR

'E sez to me, "Wot's orl this flamin' war?
  The papers torks uv nothin' else but scraps.
An' wot's ole England got snake-'eaded for?
  An' wot's the strength uv callin' out our chaps?"
'E sez to me, "Struth! Don't she rule the sea?
Wot does she want wiv us?" 'e sez to me.

Ole Ginger Mick is loadin' up 'is truck
  One mornin' in the markit feelin' sore.
'E sez to me, "Well, mate, I've done me luck;
  An' Rose is arstin', 'Wot about this war?'
I'm gone a tenner at the two-up school;
The game is crook, an' Rose is turnin' cool."

'E sez to me, " 'Ow is it fer a beer?"
  I tips 'im 'ow I've told me wife, Doreen,
That when I comes down to the markit 'ere
  I dodges pubs, an' chucks the tipple, clean.
Wiv 'er an' kid alone up on the farm
She's full uv fancies that I'll come to 'arm.

" 'Enpecked!" 'e sez. An' then, "Ar, I dunno.
  I wouldn't mind if I wus in yer place.
I've 'arf a mind to give cold tea a go—
  It's no game, pourin' snake-juice in yer face.
But, lad, I 'ave to, wiv the thirst I got:
I'm goin' over now to stop a pot."

'E goes acrost to find a pint a 'ome;
  An' meets a pal an' keeps another down.
Ten minutes later, when 'e starts to roam
  Back to the markit, wiv an ugly frown,
'E sprags a soljer bloke 'oo's passin' by,
An' sez 'e'd like to dot 'im in the eye.

43

E

"Your sort," sez Mick, "don't know yer silly mind!
    They lead yeh like a sheep; it's time yeh woke—
The 'eads is makin' piles out uv your kind!"
    "Aw, git yer 'ead read!" sez the soljer bloke.
'Struth! 'e wus willin' wus that Kharki chap;
I 'ad me work cut out to stop a scrap.

An' as the soljer fades acrost the street,
    Mick strikes a light an' sits down on 'is truck,
An' chews 'is fag—a sign 'is nerve is beat—
    An' swears a bit, an' sez 'e's done 'is luck.
'E grouches there ten minutes, maybe more,
Then sez quite sudden, *"Blarst the flamin' war!"*

Jist then a motor car goes glidin' by
    Wiv two fat toffs be'ind two fat cigars;
Mick twigs 'em frum the corner uv 'is eye—
    "I 'ope," 'e sez, "the 'Uns don't git *my* cars.
Me di'mon's, too, don't let me sleep a wink . . .
Ar, 'Struth! I'd fight fer that sort—I *don't* think."

                .   .   .   .

Then Mick gits up an' starts another fag.
    "Ar, well," 'e sez, "it's no affair uv mine,
If I don't work they'd pinch me on the vag;
    But I'm not keen to fight so toffs kin dine
On pickled olives . . . *Blarst* the flamin' war!
I ain't got nothin' worth the fightin' for.

"So long," 'e sez. "I got ter trade me stock;
    An' when yeh 'ear I've took a soljer's job
I give yeh leave to say I've done me block
    An' got a flock uv weevils in me knob."
An' then, orf-'anded-like, 'e arsts me: "Say,
Wot are they slingin' soljers fer their pay?"

I tells 'im; an' 'e sez to me, "So long.
    Some day this rabbit trade will git me beat."
An' Ginger Mick shoves thro' the markit throng,
    An' gits 'is barrer out into the street.
An', as 'e goes, I 'ears 'is gentle roar:
    'Rabbee! Wile Rabbee! . . . Blarst the flamin' war!"

44

THE CALL OF STOUSH

Wot price ole Ginger Mick? 'E's done a break—
    Gone to the flamin' war to stoush the foe.
Wus it fer glory, or a woman's sake?
    Ar, arst me somethin' easy! I dunno.
'Is Kharki clobber set 'im off a treat,
That's all I know; 'is motive's got me beat.

Ole Mick 'e's trainin' up in Cairo now;
    An' all the cops in Spadger's Lane is sad.
They miss 'is music in the midnight row
    Wot time the pushes mix it good an' glad.
Fer 'e wus one o' them, you understand,
Wot "soils the soshul life uv this fair land."

'E wus a man uv vierlence, wus Mick,
    Coarse wiv 'is speech an' in 'is manner low,
Slick wiv 'is 'ands, an' 'andy wiv a brick
    When bricks wus needful to defeat a foe.
An' now 'e's gone an' mizzled to the war,
An' some blokes 'as the nerve to arst "Wot for?"

Why did 'e go? 'E 'ad a decent job,
    'Is tart an' 'im they could 'a' made it right.
Why does a wild bull fight to guard the mob?
    Why does a bloomin' bull-ant look fer fight?
Why does a rooster scrap an' flap an' crow?
'E went becos 'e dam well 'ad to go.

'E never spouted no 'igh-soundin' stuff
    About stern jooty an' 'is country's call;
But, in 'is way, 'e 'eard it right enough
    A-callin' like the shout uv "On the Ball!"
Wot time the footer brings the clicks great joy,
An' Saints or Carlton roughs it up wiv 'Roy.

The call wot came to cave-men in the days
   When rocks wus stylish in the scrappin' line;
The call wot knights 'eard in the minstrel's lays,
   That sent 'em in tin soots to Palerstine;
The call wot draws all fighters to the fray
It come to Mick, an' Mick 'e must obey . . .

Be'ind that dile uv 'is, as 'ard as sin,
   Wus strange, soft thorts that never yet showed out;
An' down in Spadger's Lane, in dirt an' din,
   'E dreamed sich dreams as poits sing about.
'E's 'ad 'is visions uv the Bonzer Tart;
An' stoushed some coot to ease 'is swellin' 'eart.

Lovin' an' fightin' . . . when the tale is told,
   That's all there is to it; an' in their way
Them brave an' noble 'ero blokes uv old
   Wus Ginger Micks—the crook 'uns uv their day.
Jist let the Call uv Stoush give 'im 'is chance
An' Ginger Mick's the 'ero of Romance.

So Ginger Mick 'e's mizzled to the war;
   Joy in 'is 'eart, an' wild dreams in 'is brain;
Gawd 'elp the foe that 'e goes gunnin' for
   If tales is true they tell in Spadger's Lane—
Tales that ud fairly freeze the gentle 'earts
Uv them 'oo knits 'is socks—the Culchered Tarts.

THE PUSH

Becos a crook done in a prince, an' narked an Emperor,
    An' struck a light that set the world aflame;
Becos the bugles East an' West sooled on the dawgs o' war,
    A bloke called Ginger Mick 'as found 'is game—
Found 'is game an' found 'is brothers, 'oo wus strangers in 'is sight,
Till they shed their silly clobber an' put on the duds fer fight.

'E 'as struck it fer a moral. Ginger's found 'is game at last,
    An' 'e's took to it like ducklin's take to drink;
An' 'is slouchin' an' 'is grouchin' an' 'is loafin' uv the past—
    'E's done wiv 'em, an' dumped 'em down the sink.
'E's a bright an' shinin' sample uv a the'ry that I 'old:
That ev'ry 'eart that ever pumped is good fer chunks o' gold.

Ev'ry feller is a gold mine if yeh take an' work 'im right:
    It is shinin' on the surface now an' then;
An' there's some is easy sinkin', but there's some wants dynermite,
    Fer they looks a 'opeless prospect—yet they're men.
An' Ginger—'ard-shell Ginger's showin' signs that 'e will pay;
But it took a flamin' world-war fer to blarst 'is crust away.

But they took 'im an' they drilled 'im an' they shipped 'im overseas
    Wiv a crowd uv blokes 'e never met before.
'E rowed wiv 'em, an' scrapped wiv 'em, an' done some tall C.B.'s,
    An' 'e lobbed wiv 'em on Egyp's sandy shore.
Then Pride o' Race lay 'olt on 'im, an' Mick shoves out 'is chest
To find 'imself Australian an' blood brothers wiv the rest.

So I gits some reel good readin' in the letter wot 'e sent—
    Tho' the spellin's pretty rotten now an' then.
"I 'ad the joes at first," 'e sez; "but now I'm glad I went,
    Fer it's fine to be among reel, livin' men.
An' it's grand to be Australian, an' to say it good an' loud
When yeh bump a forrin country wiv sich fellers as our crowd.

47

" 'Struth! I've 'ung around me native land fer close on thirty year,
    An' I never knoo wot men me cobbers were:
Never knoo that toffs wus white men till I met 'em over 'ere—
    Blokes an' coves I sort o' snouted over there.
Yes, I loafed aroun' me country; an' I never knoo 'er then;
But the reel, ribuck Australia's 'ere, among the fightin' men.

"We've slung the swank fer good an' all; it don't fit in our plan;
    To skite uv birth an' boodle is a crime.
A man wiv us, why, 'e's a man becos 'e is a man,
    An' a reel red-'ot Australian ev'ry time.
Fer dawg an' side an' snobbery is down an' out fer keeps.
It's grit an' reel good fellership that gits yeh friends in 'eaps.

"There's a bloke 'oo shipped when I did; 'e wus lately frum 'is ma.
    'Oo 'ad filled 'im full uv notions uv 'is birth;
An' 'e overworked 'is aitches till 'e got the loud 'Ha-ha
    Frum the fellers, but 'e wouldn't come to earth.
I bumped 'is lordship, name o' Keith, an' 'ad a little row,
An' 'e lost some chunks uv beauty; but 'e's good Australian now.

"There is Privit Snifty Thompson, 'oo wus once a Sydney rat,
    An' 'e 'ung around the Rocks when 'e wus young.
There's little Smith uv Collin'wood, wiv fags stuck in 'is 'at,
    An' a string uv dirty insults on 'is tongue.
A corperil took them in 'and—a lad frum Lameroo.
Now both is nearly gentlemen, an' good Australians too.

"There's one, 'e doesn't tork a lot, 'e sez 'is name is Trent,
    Jist a privit, but 'e knows 'is drill a treat;
A stand-orf bloke, but reel good pals wiv fellers in 'is tent,
    But 'is 'ome an' 'istoree 'as got 'em beat.
They reckon when 'e starts to bleed 'e'll stain 'is Kharki blue;
An' 'is lingo smells uv Oxford—but 'e's good Australian too.

"Then there's Lofty Craig uv Queensland, 'oo's a special pal uv
    mine;
    Slow an' shy, an' kind o' nervous uv 'is height;
An' Jupp, 'oo owns a copper show, an' arsts us out to dine

When we're doo fer leave in Cairo uv a night.
An' there's Bills an' Jims an' Bennos, an' there's Roys an' 'Arolds too,
An' they're cobbers, an' they're brothers, an' Australians thro' an'
    thro'.

"There is farmers frum the Mallee, there is bushmen down frum
    Bourke,
    There's college men wiv letters to their name;
There is grafters, an' there's blokes 'oo never done a 'ard day's work
    Till they tumbled, wiv the rest, into the game—
An' they're drillin' 'ere together, men uv ev'ry creed an' kind
It's Australia! Solid! Dinkum! that 'as left the land be'ind.

"An' if yeh want a slushy, or a station overseer,
    Or a tinker, or a tailor, or a snob,
Or a 'andy bloke wiv 'orses, or a minin' ingineer,
    Why, we've got the very man to do yer job.
Butcher, baker, undertaker, or a Caf' de Pary chef,
'E is waitin', keen an' ready, in the little A.I.F.

"An' they've drilled us. Strike me lucky! but they've drilled us fer
    a cert!
    We 'ave trod around ole Egyp's burnin' sand
Till I tells meself at evenin', when I'm wringin' out me shirt,
    That we're built uv wire an' green-'ide in our land.
Strike! I thort I knoo 'ard yakker, w'ish I've tackled many ways,
But uv late I've took a tumble I bin dozin' orl me days.

"It's a game, lad," writes ole Ginger, "it's a game I'm likin' grand,
    An' I'm tryin' fer a stripe to fill in time;
I 'ave took a pull on shicker fer the honour uv me land,
    An' I'm umpty round the chest an' feelin' prime.
Yeh kin tell Rose, if yeh see 'er, I serloots 'er o'er the foam,
An' we'll 'ave a cray fer supper when I comes a'marchin' 'ome."

So ole Ginger sends a letter, an' 'is letter's good to read,
    Fer the things 'e sez, an' some things 'e leaves out;
An' when a bloke like 'im wakes up an' starts to take a 'eed,
    Well, it's sort o' worth the writin' 'ome about.
'E's one uv many little things Australia chanced to find
She never knoo she 'ad around till bugles cleared 'er mind.

Becos ole Europe lost 'er block an' started 'eavin' bricks,
  Becos the bugles wailed a song uv war,
We found reel gold down in the 'earts uv orl our Ginger Micks
  We never thort worth minin' fer before.
An' so, I'm tippin' we will pray, before our win is scored:
"Thank God fer Mick, an' Bill an' Jim, an' little brother Clord."

THE SINGING SOLDIERS

"When I'm sittin' in me dug-out wiv me rifle on me knees,
An' a yowlin', 'owlin' chorus comes a-floatin' up the breeze—
    Jist a bit o' 'Bonnie Mary' or 'Long Way to Tipperary'—
Then I know I'm in Australia, took an' planted overseas.
        They've bin up agin it solid since we crossed the flamin' foam;
        But they're singin'—alwiz singin'—since we left the wharf at 'ome.

"O, it's 'On the Mississippi' or 'Me Grey 'Ome in the West'—
If it's death an' 'ell nex' minute they must git it orf their chest.
    'Ere's a snatch o' 'When yer Roamin'—When yer Roamin' in
        the Gloamin'.'
'Struth! The first time that I 'eard it, wiv me 'ead on Rosie's breast,
        We wus comin' frum a picnic in a Ferntree Gully train . . .
        But the shrapnel made the music when I 'eard it sung again."

So I gits it straight frum Ginger in 'is letter 'ome to me,
On a dirty scrap o' paper wiv the writin' 'ard to see.
    "Strike!" sez 'e. "It sounds like skitin'; but they're singin' while
        they're fightin';
An' they socks it into Abdul to the toon o' 'Nancy Lee'.
        An' I seen a bloke this mornin' wiv 'is arm blown to a rag,
        'Ummin' 'Break the Noos to Mother', w'ile 'e sucked a soothin'
            fag.

"Now, the British Tommy curses, an' the French does fancy stunts,
An' the Turk 'e 'owls to Aller, an' the Gurkha grins an' grunts;
    But our boys is singin', singin', while the blinded shells is flingin'
Mud an' death inter the trenches in them 'eavens called the Fronts.
        An' I guess their souls keep singin' when they gits the tip to
            go . . ."
So I gits it, straight frum Ginger; an', Gawstruth! 'e ort to know.

An' 'is letter gits me thinkin' when I read sich tales as these,
An' I takes a look around me at the paddicks an' the trees;
    When I 'ears the thrushes trillin', when I 'ear the magpies fillin'
All the air frum earth to 'eaven wiv their careless melerdies—
        It's the sunshine uv the country, caught an' turned to bonzer notes;
        It's the sunbeams changed to music pourin' frum a thousand
            throats.

51

Can a soljer 'elp 'is singin' when 'e's born in sich a land?
Wiv the sunshine an' the music pourin' out on ev'ry 'and;
  Where the very air is singin', an' each breeze that blows is
    bringin'
'Armony an' mirth an' music fit to beat the blazin' band.
    On the march, an' in the trenches, when a swingin' chorus starts,
    They are pourin' bottled sunshine of their 'Omeland frum their
      'earts . . .

When they socked it to the *Southland* wiv our sunny boys aboard—
Them that stopped a dam torpeder, an' a knock-out punch wus
    scored;
  Tho' their 'ope o' life grew murky, wiv the ship 'ead over turkey,
Dread o' death an' fear o' drownin' wus jist trifles they ignored.
    They spat out the blarsted ocean, an' they filled 'emselves wiv air,
    An' they passed along the chorus of "Australia will be There".

Yes, they sung it in the water; an' a bloke aboard a ship
Sez 'e *knoo* they wus Australians be the way they give it lip—
  Sung it to the soothin' motion of the dam devourin' ocean
Like a crowd o' seaside trippers in to 'ave a little dip.
    When I 'eard that tale, I tell yeh, straight, I sort o' felt a choke;
    Fer I seemed to 'ear 'em singin', an' I know that sort o' bloke.

Yes, I know 'im; so I seen 'im, barrackin' Eternity.
An' the land that 'e wus born in is the land that mothered me.
  Strike! I ain't no sniv'lin' blighter; but I own me eyes git brighter
When I see 'em pokin' mullock at the everlastin' sea:
    When I 'ear 'em mockin' terror wiv a merry slab o' mirth,
    'Ell! I'm proud I bin to *gaol* in sich a land as give 'em birth!

· · · · · · ·

"When I'm sittin' in me dug-out wiv the bullets droppin' near,"
Writes ole Ginger; "an' a chorus smacks me in the flamin' ear:
  P'raps a song that Rickards billed, er p'raps a line o' 'Waltz
    Matilder',
Then I feel I'm in Australia, took an' shifted over 'ere.
    Till the music sort o' gits me, an' I lets me top notes roam
    While I treats the gentle foeman to a chunk uv ' 'Ome, Sweet
      'Ome'."

They wus singin' on the troopship, they wus singin' in the train;
When they left their land be'ind 'em they wus shoutin' a refrain,
    An' I'll bet they 'ave a chorus, gay an' glad in greetin' for us,
When their bit uv scrappin's over, an' they lob back 'ome again . . .
    An' the blokes that ain't returnin'—blokes that's paid the biggest
        price—
    They'll go singin', singin', singin' to the Gates uv Paradise.

A LETTER TO THE FRONT

I 'AVE written Mick a letter in reply to one uv 'is,
Where 'e arsts 'ow things is goin' where the gums an' wattles is.
So I tries to buck 'im up a bit; to go fer Abdul's fez;
An' I ain't no nob at litrachure; but this is wot I sez:

I suppose you fellers dream, Mick, in between the scraps out there,
Uv the land yeh left be'ind yeh when yeh sailed to do yer share:
Uv Collins Street, or Rundle Street, or Pitt, or George, or Hay,
Uv the land beyond the Murray or along the Castlereagh.
An' I guess yeh dream of old days an' the things yeh used to do,
An' yeh wonder 'ow 'twill strike yeh when yeh've seen this business
    thro';
An' yeh try to count yer chances when yeh've finished wiv the Turk
An' swap the gaudy war game fer a spell o' plain, drab work.

Well, Mick, yeh know jist 'ow it is these early days o' Spring,
When the gildin' o' the wattle chucks a glow on ev'rything:
Them olden days, the golden days that you remember well,
In spite o' war an' worry, Mick, are wiv us fer a spell.
Fer the green is on the paddicks, an' the sap is in the trees.
An' the bush birds in the gullies sing the ole, sweet melerdies;
An' we're 'opin', as we 'ear 'em, that, when next the Springtime
    comes,
You'll be wiv us 'ere to listen to that bird-tork in the gums.

It's much the same ole Springtime, Mick, yeh reckerlect uv yore;
Boronier an' dafferdils and wattle blooms once more
Sling sweetness over city streets, an' seem to put to shame
The rotten greed an' butchery that got you on this game—
The same ole sweet September days, an' much the same ole place;
Yet, there's a sort o' *somethin'*, Mick, upon each passin' face—
A sort o' look that's got me beat; a look that you put there,
The day yeh lobbed upon the beach an' charged at Sari Bair . . .

There's bin a lot o' tork, ole mate, uv wot we owe to you,
An' wot yeh've braved an' done fer us, an' wot we mean to do.
We've 'ailed you boys as 'eroes, Mick, an' torked uv just reward
When you 'ave done the job yer at an' slung aside the sword.
I guess it makes yeh think a bit, an' weigh this gaudy praise;
Fer even 'eroes 'ave to eat, an'—there is other days:
The days to come when we don't need no bonzer boys to fight:
When the flamin' picnic's over an' the Leeuwin looms in sight.

Then there's another fight to fight, an' you will find it tough
To sling the Kharki clobber fer the plain civilian stuff.
When orl the cheerin' dies away, an' 'ero-worship flops,
Yeh'll 'ave to face the ole tame life—'ard yakker or 'ard cops.
But, lad, yer land is wantin' yeh, an' wantin' each strong son
To fight the fight that never knows the firin' uv a gun:
The steady fight, when orl you boys will show wot you are worth,
An' punch a cow on Yarra Flats or drive a quill in Perth.

The gilt is on the wattle, Mick, young leaves is on the trees,
An' the bush birds in the gullies swap the ole sweet melerdies;
There's a good, green land awaitin' you when you come 'ome again
To swing a pick at Ballarat or ride Yarrowie Plain.
The streets is gay wiv dafferdils—but, haggard in the sun,
A wounded soljer passes; an' we know ole days is done;
Fer somew'ere down inside us, lad, is somethin' you put there
The day yeh swung a dirty left, fer us, at Sari Bair.

RABBITS

"Ar! Gimme fights wiv foemen I kin see,
　To upper-cut an' wallop on the jor.
Life in a burrer ain't no good to me.
　　　　　'Struth! This ain't war!
Gimme a ding-dong go fer 'arf a round,
An' you kin 'ave this crawlin' underground.

"Gimme a ragin', 'owlin', tearin' scrap,
　Wiv room to swing me left, an' feel it land.
This 'idin', sneakin' racket makes a chap
　　　　　Feel secon'-'and.
Stuck in me dug-out 'ere, down in a 'ole,
I'm feelin' like I've growed a rabbit's soul."

Ole Ginger's left the 'orspital, it seems;
　'E's back at Anzac, cursin' at the game;
Fer this 'ere ain't the fightin' uv 'is dreams;
　　　　　It's too dead tame.
'E's got the oopizootics reely bad,
An' 'idin' in a burrer makes 'im mad.

'E sort o' takes it personal, yeh see.
　'E used to 'awk 'em fer a crust, did Mick.
Now, makin' *'im* play rabbits seems to be
　　　　　A narsty trick.
To shove 'im like a bunny down a 'ole
It looks like chuckin' orf, an' sours 'is soul.

"Fair doos," 'e sez, "I joined the bloomin' ranks
　To git away frum rabbits: thinks I'm done
Wiv them Australian pests, an' 'ere's their thanks:
　　　　　They makes me one!
An' 'ere I'm squattin', scared to shift about;
Jist waitin' fer me little tail to sprout.

56

"Ar, strike me up a wattle! but it's tough!
   But 'ere s the dizzy limit, fer a cert—
To live this bunny's life is bad enough,
         But 'ere's reel dirt:
Some tart at 'ome 'as sent, wiv lovin' care,
A coat uv rabbit-skins fer me to wear!

"That's done it! Now I'm nibblin' at me food,
   An' if a dawg shows up I'll start to squeal;
I s'pose I orter melt wiv gratichude:
         'Tain't 'ow I feel.
She might 'a' fixed a note on wiv a pin:
'Please, Mister Rabbit, yeh fergot yer skin!'

"I sees me finish! . . . War? Why, this ain't war!
   It's ferritin'! An' I'm the bloomin' game.
Me skin alone is worth the 'untin' for—
         That tart's to blame!
Before we're done, I've got a silly scare,
Some trappin' Turk will catch me in a snare.

" 'E'll skin me, wiv the others 'e 'as there,
   An' shove us on a truck, an' bung us 'round
Constantinople at a bob a pair—
         Orl fresh an' sound!
'Eads down, 'eels up, 'e'll 'awk us in a row
Around the 'arems, 'owlin' 'Rabbee-oh!'

"But, dead in earnest, it's a job I 'ate.
   We've got to do it, an' it's gittin' done;
But this soul-dopin' game uv sit-an'-wait,
         It ain't no fun.
There's times I wish, if we weren't short uv men,
That I wus back in 'orspital again.

"Ar, 'orspital! There is the place to git.
   If I thort Paradise wus 'arf so snug
I'd shove me 'ead above the parapit
         An' stop a slug;
But one thing blocks me playin' sich a joke:
I want another scrap before I croak.

"I want it bad. I want to git right out
    An' plug some josser in the briskit—'ard.
I want to 'owl an' chuck me arms about,
                An' jab, an' guard,
An' swing, an' upper-cut, an' crool some pitch,
Or git passed out meself—I don't care w'ich.

            .   .   .   .   .   .

"I'm sittin' in me dug-out day be day—
    It narks us; but Australia's got a name
Fer doin' little jobs like blokes 'oo play
                A clean straight game.
Wiv luck I might see scrappin' 'fore I'm done,
Or go where Craig 'as gone, an' miss the fun.

"But if I dodge, an' keep out uv the rain,
    An' don't toss in me alley 'fore we wins;
An' if I lobs back 'ome an' meets the Jane
                'Oo sent the skins—
These bunnies' overcoats I lives inside—
I'll squeal at 'er, an' run away an' 'ide.

"But, torkin' straight, the Janes 'as done their bit.
    I'd like to 'ug the lot, orl on me pat!
They warms us well, the things they've sewed an' knit:
                An' more than that—
I'd like to tell them dear Australian tarts
The spirit uv it warms Australian 'earts."

THE GAME

"Ho! the sky's as blue as blazes an' the sun is shinin' bright,
   An' the dicky birds is singin' over'ead,
An' I'm 'ummin', softly 'ummin', w'ile I'm achin' fer a fight,
   An' the chance to fill some blighter full of lead.
An' the big guns they are boomin', an' the shells is screamin' past,
But I'm corperil—lance-corperil—an' found me game at last!"

I ixpects a note frum Ginger, fer the time wus gettin' ripe,
   An' I gits one thick wiv merry 'owls uv glee;
Fer they've gone an' made 'im corperil—they've given 'im a stripe,
   An' yeh'd think, to see 'is note, it wus V.C.
Fer 'e chortles like a nipper wiv a bran' noo Noah's Ark
Since forchin she 'as smiled on 'im, an' life's no more a nark.

"Ho! the sky along the 'ill-tops, it is smudged wiv cannon smoke,
   An' the shells along the front is comin' fast,
But the 'eads 'ave 'ad the savvy fer to reckernise a bloke,
   An' permotion's gettin' common-sense at last.
An' they picked me fer me manners, w'ich wus snouted over 'ome,
But I've learned to be a soljer since I crossed the ragin' foam.

"They 'ave picked me 'cos they trust me; an' it's got me where I live,
   An' it's put me on me mettle, square an' all;
I wusn't in the runnin' once when blokes 'ad trust to give,
   But over 'ere I answers to the call;
So some shrewd 'ead 'e marked me well, an' when the time wus ripe
'E took a chance on Ginger Mick, an' I 'ave snared me stripe.

"I've got a push to 'andle now wot makes a soljer proud—
   Yeh ort to see the boys uv my ole squad:
The willin'est, the cheeriest, don'-care-a-damest crowd,
   An' the toughest ever seen outside o' quod.
I reckon that they gimme 'em becos they wus so meek,
But they know me, an' they understan' the lingo that I speak.

F

"So I'm a little corperil, wiv pretties on me arm,
  But yeh'd never guess it fer to see me now,
Fer me valet 'e's been careless an' me trooso's come to 'arm,
  An' me pants want creasin' badly I'll allow.
But to see me squad in action is a cure fer sandy blight,
They are shy on table manners, but they've notions 'ow ter fight.

"There's a little picnic promised that 'as long been overdoo,
  An' we're waitin' fer the order to advance;
An' me bones is fairly achin' fer to see my boys bung thro',
  Fer I know they're dancin' mad to git the chance.
An' there's some'll sure be missin' when we git into the game;
But if they lorst their corperil 'twould be a cryin' shame.

"When it's gettin' near to evenin' an' the guns is slowin' down
  I fergits the playful 'abits uv our foes,
An' finds meself a-thinkin' thorts uv good ole Melbourne town,
  An' dreamin' dilly dreams about ole Rose.
O' course I'll see me girl again, an' give a clean, square deal,
When I come smilin' 'ome again . . . But that ain't 'ow I feel.

"I feel . . . I dunno 'ow I feel. I feel that things is done.
  I seem t've 'it the limit in some way.
Per'aps I'm orf me pannikin wiv sittin' in the sun,
  But I jist wrote to Rose the other day;
An' I wrote 'er sort o' mournful 'cos—I dunno 'ow it seems . . .
Ar, I'm a gay galoot to go an' 'ave these dilly dreams!

"Wot price the bran' noo corperil, wiv sof'nin' uv the 'eart!
  If my pet lambs thort me a turtle dove
I'd 'ave to be reel stern wiv 'em, an' make another start
  To git 'em where I got 'em jist wiv love . . .
But don't fergit, if you or your Doreen sees Rose about,
Jist tell 'er that I'm well an' strong, an' sure uv winnin' out.

"*Ho! the sky's as blue as blazes, an' the sun is shinin' still,*
  An' the dicky bird is perchin' on the twig,
An' the guns is pop, pop, poppin' frum the trenches on the 'ill,
  An' I'm lookin' bonny in me non-com's rig.
An' when yer writin' me again—don't think I want ter skite—
But don't fergit the 'Corperil'; an' mind yeh spells it right."

"A GALLANT GENTLEMAN"

A MONTH ago the world grew grey fer me;
   A month ago the light went out fer Rose.
To 'er they broke it gentle as might be;
   But fer 'is pal 'twus one uv them swift blows
That stops the 'eart-beat; fer to me it came
Jist, "Killed in Action", an', beneath, *'is* name.

'Ow many times 'ave I sat dreamin' 'ere
   An' seen the boys returnin', gay an' proud.
I've seen the greetin's, 'eard 'is rousin' cheer,
   An' watched ole Mick come stridin' thro' the crowd.
'Ow many times 'ave I sat in this chair
An' seen 'is 'ard chiv grinnin' over there.

'E's laughed, an' told me stories uv the war.
   Changed some 'e looked, but still the same ole **Mick,**
Keener an' cleaner than 'e wus before;
   'E's took me 'and, an' said 'e's in great nick.
Sich wus the dreamin's uv a fool 'oo tried
To jist crack 'ardy, an' 'old gloom aside.

An' now—well, wot's the odds? I'm only one;
   One out uv many 'oo 'as lost a friend.
Manlike, I'll bounce again, an' find me fun;
   But fer poor Rose it seems the bitter end.
Fer Rose, an' sich as Rose, when one man dies
It seems the world goes black before their eyes.

A parson cove he broke the noos to Rose—
   A friend uv mine, a bloke wiv snowy 'air
An' gentle, soothin' sort o' ways, 'oo goes
   Thro' life jist 'umpin' others' loads uv care.
Instid uv Mick—jist one rough soljer lad—
Yeh'd think 'e'd lost the dearest friend 'e 'ad.

But 'ow kin blows be sof'n'd sich as that?
   Rose took it as 'er sort must take sich things.
An' if the jolt uv it 'as knocked me flat,
   Well, 'oo is there to blame 'er if it brings
Black thorts that comes to women when they frets,
An' makes 'er tork wild tork an' foolish threats?

An' then there comes the letter that wus sent
   To give the strength uv Ginger's passin' out—
A long, straight letter frum a bloke called Trent;
   'Tain't no use tellin' wot it's orl about:
There's things that's in it I kin see quite clear
Ole Ginger Mick ud be ashamed to 'ear.

Things praisin' 'im, that pore ole Mick ud say
   Wus comin' it too 'ot; fer, spare me days!
I well remember that 'e 'ad a way
   Uv curlin' up when 'e wus slung bokays.
An' Trent 'e seems to think that in some way
'E owes Mick somethin' that 'e can't repay.

Well, p'raps 'e does; an' in the note 'e sends
   'E arsts if Mick 'as people 'e kin find.
Fer Trent's an English toff wiv swanky friends,
   An' wants to 'elp wot Ginger's left be'ind.
'E sez strange things in this 'ere note 'e sends:
"He was a gallant gentleman," it ends.

A gallant gentleman! Well, I dunno.
   I 'ardly think that Mick ud like that name.
But this 'ere Trent's a toff, an' ort to know
   The breedin' uv the stock frum which 'e came.
Gallant an' game Mick might 'a' bin; but then—
Lord! Fancy 'im among the gentlemen!

The way 'e died . . . Gawd! but it makes me proud
   I ever 'eld 'is 'and, to read that tale.
An' Trent is one uv that 'igh-steppin' crowd
   That don't sling praise around be ev'ry mail.
To 'im it seemed some great 'eroic lurk;
But Mick, I know, jist took it wiv 'is work.

Trent tells 'ow, when they found 'im, near the end,
   'E starts a fag an' grins orl bright an' gay.
An' when they arsts fer messages to send
   To friends, 'is look goes dreamin' far away.
"Look after Rose," 'e sez, "when I move on.
Look after . . . Rose . . . Mafeesh!" An' 'e wus gone.

"We buried 'im," sez Trent, "down by the beach.
   We put mimosa on the mound uv sand
Above 'im. 'Twus the nearest thing in reach
   To golden wattle uv 'is native land.
But never wus the fairest wattle wreath
More golden than the 'eart uv 'im beneath."

A gallant gentleman . . . Well, let it go.
   They sez they've put them words above 'is 'ead,
Out there where lonely graves stretch in a row;
   But Mick 'e'll never mind it now 'e's dead.
An' where 'e's gone, when they weigh praise an' blame,
P'raps gentlemen an' men is much the same.

     .   .   .   .

A month ago, fer me the world grew grey;
   A month ago the light went out fer Rose;
Becos one common soljer crossed the way,
   Leavin' a common message as 'e goes.
But ev'ry dyin' soljer's 'ope lies there:
"Look after Rose. Mafeesh!" Gawd! It's a pray'r!

That's wot it is; an' when yeh sort it out,
   Shuttin' year ears to orl the sounds o' strife—
The shouts, the cheers, the curses—'oo kin doubt
   The claims uv women; mother, sweet'eart, wife?
An' 'oo's to 'ear our soljers' dyin' wish?
An' 'oo's to 'eed? . . . "Look after Rose . . . Mafeesh!"

DOREEN

[*A slim, illustrated booklet, Doreen was issued near the end of 1917 to serve as a Christmas gift. The example here given is representative of the four poems in the booklet. E. V. Lucas was much taken by this little work. "It contains more married love to the square inch," he said, "than anything I have ever read."*]

WASHING DAY

The little gipsy vi'lits, they wus peepin' thro' the green
As she come walkin' in the grass, me little wife, Doreen.
   The sun shone on the sassafras, where thrushes sung a bar;
   The 'ope an' worry uv our lives was yellin' fer 'is Mar.
I watched 'er comin' down the green; the sun wus on 'er 'air—
Jist the woman that I marri'd, when me luck wus 'eadin' fair.

I seen 'er walkin' in the sun that lit our little farm:
She 'ad three clothes-pegs in 'er mouth, an' washin' on 'er arm—
   Three clothes-pegs, fer I counted 'em, an' watched 'er as she come;
   "The stove-wood's low," che mumbles, "an' young Bill 'as cut 'is
      thumb."
Now, it weren't no giddy love-speech, but it seemed to take me
      straight
Back to the time I kissed 'er first beside 'er mother's gate.

Six years uv wedded life we've 'ad, an' still me dreams is sweet . . .
Aw, them bonzer little vi'lits, they wus smilin' round me feet.
   An' wot's a bit uv stove-wood count, wiv paddicks grinnin' green,
   When a bloke gits on to dreamin' uv the old days an' Doreen—
The days I thort I snared a saint; but since I've understood
I 'ave wed a dinkum woman, which is fifty times as good.

I 'ave wed a dinkum woman, an' she's give me eyes to see—
Oh, I ain't been mollycoddled, an' there ain't no fluff on me!
   But days when I wus down an' out she seemed so 'igh above;
   An' a saint is made fer worship, but a woman's made fer love.
An' a bloke is growin' richer as sich things 'e comes to know . . .
(She pegs another sheet an' sez, "The stove-wood's gittin' low.")

A bloke 'e learns a lot uv things in six years wiv a tart;
But thrushes in the sassafras ain't singin' like me 'eart.
   'Tis the thrushes 'oo 'ave tort me in their choonful sort o' way
   That it's best to take things singin' as yeh meet 'em day be day;
Fer I wed a reel, live woman, wiv a woman's 'appy knack
Uv torkin' reason inside out an' logic front to back.

An' I like it. 'Struth, I like it! Fer a wax doll in a 'ome,
She'd give a man the flamin' pip an' longin's fer to roam.
  Aw, I ain't no silk-sock sonkie 'oo ab'ors the rood an' rough;
  Fer, city-born an' gutter-bred, me schoolin' it wus tough.
An' I like the dinkum woman 'oo . . . (She jerks the clothes-prop, so,
An' sez, so sweet an' dangerous, "The stove-wood's gittin' low.")

See, I've studied men in cities, an' I've studied 'em out 'ere;
I've seen 'em 'ard thro' piety an' seen 'em kind thro' beer.
  I've seen the meanest doin' deeds to make the angels smile,
  An' watched the proudest playin' games that crooks 'ud reckon
    vile.
I 'ave studied 'em in bunches, an' I've read 'em one be one,
An' there isn't much between 'em when the 'ole thing's said an'
  done.

An' I've sort o' studied wimmin—fer I've met a tidy few—
An' there's times, when I wus younger, when I kids meself I knew.
  But 'im 'oo 'opes to count the stars or measure up the sea,
  'E kin 'ave a shot at woman, fer she's fairly flummoxed me . . .
("I'll 'ave to 'ave *some* wood," she sez, an' sez it most perlite
An' secret to a pair uv socks; an' jams a peg in, tight.)

Now, a woman, she's a woman. I 'ave fixed that fer a cert.
They're jist as like as rows uv peas from 'at to 'em uv skirt.
  An' then, they're all so different, yeh find, before yeh've done,
  The more yeh know uv all uv 'em the less yeh know uv one.
An' then, the more yeh know uv one . . . (She gives 'er 'air a touch:
"The stove-wood's nearly done," she sez. "Not that it matters *much!*")

The little gipsy vi'lits, they wus smilin' round me feet.
An' this dreamin' dilly day-dreams on a Summer day wus sweet.
  I 'eaves me frame frum orf the fence, an' grabs me little axe;
  But, when I'm 'arf way to the shed, she stops me in me tracks.
"Yer lunch is ready. That ole wood kin easy wait a while."
Strike! I'm marri'd to a woman . . . But she never seen me smile.

ROSE OF SPADGERS

[*After causing the Sentimental Bloke and company to appear in three books and a booklet between 1915 and 1919, Dennis appeared to have exhausted his rich vein. Five years later, however, he tapped it again, producing then a series of verse-tales relating to the experiences of Rose, the girl who was bereft by the death of Ginger Mick. Five of the 16 episodes in the book are given here. They describe the "'oly war" that brought about Rose's rescue and give an indication of how she became regenerated on the Bloke's farm. Although this book, the last in the Bloke medium, was not as successful as its predecessors, it contains some vivid and amusing material. Also, it provides another illustration of the deftness of Dennis in raising an earlier minor character to eminence in a later work.*]

THE FALTERING KNIGHT

It knocks me can in, this 'ere game uv life,
　　A bloke gets born, grows up, looks round fer fun,
Dreams dilly dreams, then wakes to find a wife
　　An' fambly round 'im—all 'is young days done.
An', gazin' back, sees in 'is youth a man
Scarce reckernised. It fair knocks in me can!

Ther's me. I never seemed to mark no change
　　As I mooched on through life frum year to year;
An' yet, at times it seems to me dead strange
　　That me, uv old, is me, 'oo's sittin' 'ere.
Per'aps it ain't. 'E was a crook young coot,
While I'm a sturdy farmer, growin' froot.

But, all the same, 'e wouldn't back an' fill,
　　An' argue with 'imself, an' 'esitate,
Once 'e 'ad seen the way. 'E'd find the will
　　To go an' do the thing 'e 'ad to, straight.
That's 'ow I was; an' now—Ar, strike a light!
Life gits so mixed I can't git nothin' right. . . .

All marrid blokes will un'erstand me well.
　　I ain't addressin' no remarks to those
'Oo've learnt but 'arf uv life. The things I tell
　　Is fer the ears uv fellermen that *knows*:
Them symperthetic 'usbands 'oo 'ave 'eard
The fog-'orn soundin' in the wifely word.

Fer when stern jooty grips a 'usband's 'eart
　　(That's me) an' eggs 'im on to start a scene
That's like to tear two 'appy lives apart,
　　In spite uv all 'er carin' (That's Doreen)
Why, there you 'ave a story that would make
A bonzer movie—with a bit uv fake.

But 'ere's the plot. When my pal, Ginger Mick,
    Chucked in 'is alley in this war we won,
'E left things tangled; fer 'e went too quick
    Fer makin' last requests uv anyone.
'E jist sez to the world, when last 'e spoke,
"Look after Rose!" . . . 'E was a trustful bloke.

Rose lives in Spadgers Lane. She lived, them days,
    Fer Mick's returnin'. When 'e never came,
If she lost 'old, an' took to careless ways,
    Well, I ain't sayin' she was much to blame.
An' I don't worry, till I 'ear she's took,
Or thinks uv takin' on to ways that's crook.

Although I'm vegetatin' on a farm,
    I gets a city whisper now an' then.
An' when I 'ear she's like to come to 'arm
    Amongst a push uv naughty spieler men,
I gets the wind up. This is all I see:
Mick was my cobber; so it's up to me.

That's all I see, quite clear, with my two eyes.
    But marrid blokes will understand once more,
When I remarks that marrid blokes is wise
    'Oo 'ave the sense to take a squint through four.
Four eyes is needed in reviewin' plans—
Their vision's broader than a single man's.

But when them four eyes sees two ways at once—
    Gets crossed—Ar, well, ther's things in marrid life
For which a hint's enough fer any dunce.
    Ther's certin things between a man an' wife
That can't be quite—But take this fer a fack:
Don't start things uv a mornin'. It ain't tack.

That was me first bad break. I should 'ave seen
    The supper things washed up, an' 'elped a bit,
An' then 'ave broke it gently to Doreen,
    Promiscus, like I jist 'ad thought uv it.
But I done worse. I blurts wot I'd to say
Upon the mornin' uv a *washin'* day!

72

I owns me ta'tic's crook. But, all the same,
   Ther' weren't no need fer certin things she said.
Wantin' to do good acts don't call fer blame,
   Even on tackless 'usban's, eight years wed.
A bloke 'oo jist suggests a 'armless plan
Don't need remindin' 'e's a *marrid* man.

'Struth! Don't I know it? Can I well ferget
   While I still 'ave two 'ealthy ears to 'ark?
Not that she torks an' mags a lot; but yet
   Ther's somethin' in 'er choice uv a remark
That gets there, worse than yappin' all day long,
An' makes me pure intentions look dead wrong.

It seems it ain't right fer a marrid bloke
   To rescue maids. I starts to answer back;
But got took up before I 'ardly spoke,
   An' innercent designs is painted black.
I calls attention to the knights uv old;
But tin knights an' romance jist leaves 'er cold.

I read 'er meanin' plain in 'er cool eye.
   Aw, strike! I ain't *admirin'* Rose! . . . Wot? . . . Me!
But when 'er look sez "Rats!" where's the reply
   A man can give, an' keep 'is dignity?
It can't be done. When they git on that lay,
Wise coves adjourns the meet, an' fades away.

That's wot I done. I gits out uv the 'ouse
   All dignified. An', jist to show 'er 'ow
Reel unconcerned I am, I starts to rouse
   Me neighbour, Wally Free, about 'is cow
Wot's got in to me cabbages, an' et
Close on a row uv 'em. I'll shoot 'er yet!

(A batchelor 'e is, this Wally Free—
   A soljer bloke that come this way last year
An' took the little farm nex' door to me.)
   When I gets mad, 'e grins frum ear to ear,
An' sez, "Cool orf," 'e sez. "It's plain your wool
'As been pulled 'ard this mornin'." 'E's a fool!

73

If 'e don't mend that fence . . . Ar, wot's the good?
   I lets 'im go, an' sneaks be'ind the shed,
An' sits there broodin' on a pile uv wood. . . .
   Ther's certin things she might 'ave left unsaid.
Ther' wasn't nothin' fer to make 'er go
An' dig up chance remarks uv years ago.

Me problem's this: Either I 'urts Doreen,
   By doin' things with which she don't agree,
Or lets Rose slide, an' treats me cobber mean—
   Ole Ginger Mick, 'oo 'ad no friend but me.
I ain't a ringtail; but, by gum, it's tough.
I loves me wife too much to treat 'er rough.

If I was single. . . . 'Struth! 'Oo wants to be?
   Fool batchelors can larf their silly larf,
An' kid theirselves they got a pull on me.
   I'm out uv sorts, that's all; an' more than 'arf
Inclined to give some coot a crack, right now
Fer pref'rince, some insultin' single cow!

A HOLY WAR

"Young friend!" . . . . I tries to duck, but miss the bus.
   'E sees me first, an' 'as me by the 'and.
"Young friend!" 'e sez; an' starts to make a fuss
   At meetin' me. "Why, this," 'e sez, "is grand!
   Events is workin' better than I planned.
It's Providence that I should meet you thus.
   You're jist the man," 'e sez, "to make a stand,
        An' strive for us.

"Young friend," 'e sez, "allow me to explain . . ."
   But wot 'e 'as to say too well I knows.
I got the stren'th uv it in Spadgers Lane
   Not 'arf an hour before'and, when I goes
   To see if I could pick up news uv Rose,
After that dentist let me off the chain.
   ("Painless," 'e's labelled. So 'e is, I s'pose.
        I 'ad the pain.)

"Young friend," 'e sez. I let 'im 'ave 'is say;
   Though I'm already wise to all 'e said—
The queer old parson, with 'is gentle way—
   ('E tied Doreen an' me when we was wed).
   I likes 'im, from 'is ole soft, snowy 'ead
Down to 'is boots. 'E ain't the sort to pray
        When folks needs bread.

Yeh'd think that 'e was simple as a child;
   An' so 'e is, some ways; but, by and by,
While 'e is talkin' churchy-like an' mild,
   Yeh catch a tiny twinkle in 'is eye
   Which gives the office that 'e's pretty fly
To cunnin' lurks. 'E ain't to be beguiled
   With fairy tales. An' when I've seen 'em try
        'E's only smiled.

75

G

But, all the same, I didn't want to meet
    'Is 'oly nibs jist then; fer well I knoo,
When I fell up against 'im in the street,
    'E 'ad a little job fer me to do.
    Fer I 'ad gethered up a tip or two
In Spadgers, where 'is rev'rince 'as 'is beat,
    Tryin' to make that Gorfergotten crew
            'Olesome an' sweet.

"Young friend," 'e sez, "I am beset by foes.
    The Church," 'e sez, "is in a quandary."
An' then 'e takes an' spills out all 'is woes,
    An' 'ints that this 'ere job is up to me.
    "Yer aid—per aps yer strong right arm," sez 'e,
"Is needed if we are to rescue Rose
    From wot base schemes an' wot iniquity
            Gawd only knows."

This is the sorry tale. Rose, sick, an' low
    In funds an' frien's, an' far too proud to beg,
Is gittin' sorely tempted fer to go
    Into the spielin' trade by one Spike Wegg.
    I knoo this Spike uv old; a reel bad egg,
'Oo's easy livin' is to git in tow
    Some country mug, an' pull 'is little leg
            Fer all 'is dough.

A crooked crook is Spike amongst the crooks,
    A rat, 'oo'd come the double on 'is friends;
Flash in 'is ways, but innercint in looks
    Which 'e works well fer 'is un'oly ends.
    "It's 'ard to know," sez Snowy, "why Fate sends
Sich men among us, or why Justice brooks
    Their evil ways, which they but seldom mends—
            Except in books.

"Young friend," 'e sez, "You're known in Spadgers Lane.
    You know their ways. We must seek out this man.
With 'er, pray'r an' persuasion 'ave been vain.
    I've pleaded, but she's bound to 'is vile plan.
    I'd 'ave you treat 'im gently, if you can;
But if you can't, well—I need not explain."
    ('E twinkles 'ere) "I'm growin' partisan;
            I must refrain."

"Do you mean stoush?" I sez. "Fer if yeh do
    I warn yeh that a scrap might put me queer."
"Young friend," sez 'e, "I leave the means to you.
    Far be it from the Church to interfere
    With noble works." But I sez, "Now, look 'ere,
I got a wife at 'ome; you know 'er, too.
    Ther's certin things I never could make clear
            If once she knoo."

"I got a wife," I sez, "an' loves 'er well,
    Like I loves peace an' quite. An' if I goes
Down into Spadgers, raisin' merry 'ell,
    Breakin' the peace an' things account uv Rose,
    Where that might land me goodness only knows.
'Ow women sees these things no man can tell.
    I've done with stoush," I sez. "'Ard knocks an' blows
            'Ave took a spell."

"I've done with stoush," I sez. But in some place
    Deep in me 'eart a voice begun to sing;
A lurin' little voice, with motives base. . . .
    It's ten long years since I was in a ring,
    Ten years since I gave that left 'ook a swing,
Ten weary years since I pushed in a face;
    An' 'ere's a chance to 'ave a little fling
            With no disgrace.

77

"Stoush? Stoush, young friend?" 'e sez. "Where 'ave I eard
  That term? I gather it refers to strife.
But there," 'e sez, "why quarrel with a word?
  As you 'ave said, indeed, I know yer wife;
  An' should she 'ear you went where vice is rife
To battle fer the right—But it's absurd
  To look fer gallantry in modrin life.
            It's a rare bird.

"Young friend," 'e sez. An' quicker than a wink
  'Is twinklin' eyes grew sudden very grave.
"Young friend," 'e sez, "I know jist wot yeh think
  Uv 'ow us parsons blather an' be'ave.
  But I 'ave 'ere a woman's soul to save—
A lonely woman, tremblin' on the brink
  Uv black perdition, blacker than the grave.
            An' she must sink.

"Yes, she must sink," 'e sez. "For I 'ave done
  All that a man uv my poor parts can do.
An' I 'ave failed! There was not anyone
  That I could turn to, till I met with you.
  But now *that* 'ope 'as gone—an' 'er 'ope too."
"'Old on," I sez. "Just let me think for one
  Brief 'arf-a-mo. I'd love a crack or two
            At this flash gun."

"Righto," I sez (an' turns me back on doubt)
  "I'm with yeh, parson. I go down to-night
To Spadgers, an' jist looks this Spike Wegg out."
  "Young friend," 'e sez, "be sure you've chosen right.
  Remember, I do not desire a fight.
But if——" "Now don't you fret," I sez, "about
  No vi'lince. If I'm forced, it will be quite
            A friendly clout."

"Young friend," 'e sez, "if you go, I go too.
  Maybe, by counsel, I may yet injuce
This evil man——" "It ain't no game for you,"
  I argues with 'im. But it ain't no use.
  "I go!" 'e sez, an' won't take no ixcuse.
So that's all fixed. An' us crusaders two
  Goes down to-night to Spadgers, to cut loose
      Till all is blue.

'Ow can Doreen make trouble or git sore?
  (Already I can 'ear 'er scold an' sob)
But this ain't stoushin'. It's a 'oly war!
  The blessin' uv the Church is on the job.
  I'm a church-worker, with full leave to lob
A sacrid left on Spike Wegg's wicked jor.
  Jist let me! Once! An' after, s'elp me bob,
      Never no more!

THE CRUSADERS

"PETER the 'Ermit was a 'oly bloke,"
  The parson sez, "wot chivvied coves to war."
  "Too right," I chips. "I've 'eard that yarn before."
"Brave knights sprung straight to arms where'er 'e spoke."
"Sure thing," sez I. "It muster been no joke
  Tinnin' yer frame in them dead days uv yore
  Before yeh starts to tap a foeman's gore."

"Peter the 'Ermit was a man inspired,"
  The parson sez. We're moochin' up the Lane,
  Snoopin' around for news we might obtain
Uv this Spike Wegg, the man 'oo I am 'ired
To snatch by 'ook or crook, jist as required
  By circs, frum out the sev'ril sins wot stain
  'Is wicked soul. I 'ope me meanin's plain.

"Peter the 'Ermit," sez the parson, "saw
  No 'arm in vi'lince when the cause was just.
  While 'e deplored, no doubt, the fightin' lust,
'E preached—" "'Old on," I sez. "'Ere comes the Law:
'Ere's Brannigan, the cop. Pos'pone the jaw
  Till we confer. I got idears 'e must
  Keep track uv Spike; if 'e toils fer 'is crust."

"Spike Wegg?" growls Brannigan. "I know that bloke;
  An' 'e's the one sweet soul I long to see.
  That shrinkin' vi'lit 'ates publicity
Jist now," sez Brannigan. "Spike Wegg's in smoke.
Oh, jist concerns a cove 'e tried to croak.
  'E's snug in some joint round about, maybe.
  If you should meet, remember 'im to me."

80

The cop passed on. "Peter the 'Ermit was
    A ri'chus man," the parson sez, "wot knoo—"
    "'Old 'ard!" I begs. "Jist for a hour or two
I wouldn't go an' nurse sich thorts, becoz
Too much soul-ferritin' might put the moz
    On this 'ere expedition. I'll 'elp you
    To search our conscience when the job is through.

"I know yer doubts," I sez, "an' 'ow you 'ate
    The thorts uv stoush, an' 'old 'ard blows in dread.
    But Pete the 'Ermit's been a long time dead.
'E'll keep. But we are in the 'ands uv Fate,
An' 'oly spruikers uv a ancient date
    Don't 'elp. I quite agrees with all you've said
    But—" "Say no more," 'e answers. "Lead ahead."

"But, all the same," 'e sez, "I want no fight."
    "Right 'ere, be'ind this 'oardin'," I replies,
    "A two-up school's in session. If we spies
About a bit, there is a chance we might
Git news—" Jist then the spotter comes to light.
    I word 'im gentle, with some 'asty lies:
    I'm seekin' Spike. See? Can 'e put me wise?

"Spike Wegg?" (At first 'e only twigs meself)
    "'E's gone—" ('E spots the parson standin' by)
    A cold, 'ard glimmer comes in 'is fish eye:
"'Ere! Wot's the game?" 'e yelps. "Are you a shelf?"
"'Ave sense!" I larfs. "I got a bit uv pelf,
    An' thort I'd like to take a little fly—"
    "Buzz orf!" 'e orders. So we done a guy.

"Blank number one," I sez. The parson sighed.
    "Joshuer fought, an' never seemed to shrink—"
    "Now, look," I tells 'im. "Honest. Don't you think
Them Bible blokes 'oo've 'ad their day an' died
Is best fergot until we're 'ome an' dried?
    Now, up the street 'ere, is a little sink
    Uv sin that does a traffic in strong drink."

"Sly grog?" 'e arsts. But I sez, " 'Ush! This place
Is kep' by Mother Weems, 'oo's sof', blue eye
An' snow-white 'air would make yeh 'shamed an' shy
To brand 'er name with any sich disgrace.
'Er kind, sweet smile, 'er innercint ole face
Beams like a blessin'. Still, we'll 'ave a try
To word the dear ole dame, an' pump 'er dry.

'Is nibs stands in the shadders while I knock.
Mother unlocks the door, an' smiles, an' peers
Into me face. She wears 'er three score years
Reel sweet, in lacy cap an' neat black frock.
Then: "Bill," she cries. "You've give me quite a shock!
Why, dearie, I ain't seen you for long years.
Come in." 'Er kind ole eyes seem close to tears.

"Dearie, come in," she chirps. But I pretend
I'm on reel urgent biz. I got to 'aste.
"Jist for ole times," she pleads. "One little taste."
"I can't," I sez. "I'm lookin' for a friend,
Spike Wegg, for 'oo I've certin news no end
Important; an' I got no time to waste."
"Wot? Spike?" she sez. "I 'ear 'e's bein' chased."

" 'E's bein' chased," she sez, "by D's, I've 'eard."
"Too true," I owns. " 'E's got no time to lose."
"Well, maybe, if you was to try Ah Foo's—
The privit room—" Then, as 'is rev'rince stirred,
She seen 'is choker. " 'Oo the 'ell's this bird?
Is this a frame?" she shrieks. . . . Without adoos,
We slap the pavemint with four 'asty shoes.

But, as along the sloppy lane we race,
'Er 'ot words tumble after in a flood:
"You pimps! You dirty swine! I'll 'ave yer blood!"
" 'Eavings!" the parson gasps. "With that sweet face!"
" 'Er words," I answer, "do seem outer place."
"Vile words, that I 'ave scarce 'arf understud."
Sez Snowy, shoshin' in a pool uv mud.

We reach Ah Foo's. "Now, 'ere," I sez, "is where
    You stop outside. Twice you 'ave put me queer
    It's a lone 'and I mean to play in 'ere.
You 'ang around an' breathe the 'olesome air."
"Young friend," 'e sez, "I go with you in there.
    I've led you into this. Why should I fear
    The danger? 'Tis me jooty to be near."

Snowy's a game un! I lob in the shop,
    The parson paddin' after on the floor.
    Ah Foo looks up. "Not there!" 'e squeaks. "Wha' for?"
But we sail past the Chow without a stop,
Straight for the little crib up near the top
    That I knoo well in sinful days uv yore. . . .
    I turn the knob; an' sling aside the door.

Beside a table, fearin' 'arm from none,
    Spike an' another bloke is teet-ah-teet.
    Quick on the knock, Spike Wegg jumps to 'is feet
An' jerks a 'and be'ind 'im for 'is gun.
I rush 'im, grab a chair up as I run,
    A' swing it with a aim that ain't too neat.
    Spike ducks aside; an', with a bump, we meet.

An' then we mix it. Strife an' merry 'ell
    Breaks loose a treat, an' things git movin' fast.
    An', as a Chinee jar goes crashin' past,
'Igh o'er the din I 'ears the parson's yell:
"Hit! Hit 'im 'ard, young friend! Chastise 'im well!
    Hit 'im!" . . . The 'oly war is in full blast;
    An' Pete the 'Ermit's come to light at last.

THE KNIGHT'S RETURN

THE conq'rin' 'ero! Me? Yes, I don't think.
  This mornin' when I catch the train fer 'ome,
It's far more like a walloped pup I slink
  To kennel, with resolves no more to roam.
Crusades is orf. I'm fer the simple life,
  'Ome with me trustin' wife
      All safe frum strife.

I've read uv knights returnin' full uv gyp,
  Back to the bewchus lady in the tower.
They never seemed to git dumestic pip
  In them brave days when knight'ood was in flower.
But times is changed; an' 'usbands 'as to 'eed;
  Fer knight'ood's run to seed;
      It 'as indeed.

Snowy, the parson, came to say farewell.
"Young friend," 'e sez, "You've did a Christian ack—
A noble deed that you'll be glad to tell
  An' boast uv to yer wife when you git back."
"Too true," I sez, reel chirpy. "She'll be proud,
  "I'll blab it to the crowd—
      If I'm allowed."

"Good-bye! Good Luck!" 'e sez. "I'll see to Rose,
  Make yer mind easy. Ierdine yer face.
Bless yeh! Good luck, young friend!" An' orf we goes—
  Me an' me conscience arguin' the case.
An', as we pick up speed an' race along,
  The rails make up a song:
      "Yer in all wrong!"

"Yer in all wrong! Yer in all wrong! Yeh blob!
    Why did yeh want to go an' 'unt fer Spike?
Yer in all wrong! Becoz yeh liked the job.
    That's wot. An' don't pretend yeh didn't like.
Yer in all wrong! Wot will yeh tell Doreen?
    Yeh'll 'ate to 'ave a scene.
        Don't yeh feel mean?"

Gawstruth, I do! It ain't so much the fack
    That I 'ave soiled me soul be breakin' trust;
But 'ere's me lip swole up an' one eye black
    An' all me map in gen'ril bunged an' bust.
'Ow can a 'omin' 'usband 'ave the neck
    To 'arf ixplain that wreck
        With self-respeck?

An' then ther's Rose. Wot 'ave I got to say
    About that invite? 'Struth! Doreen an' Rose!
Arstin' strange dames (comparative) to stay
    Ain't done since knights 'ad buttons to their clo'es.
Wot's after, if I do pull orf the coop?
    I feel me spirits droop.
        I'm in the soup!

Two stations on, a w'iskered coot gits in
    I seem to sort uv rekernise, some'ow.
But all at once I place 'im, an' I grin.
    But 'e don't jerry; 'e's stone sober now.
It's 'im I scragged in Spadgers—number one—
    The late suspected gun.
        It's Danny Dunn.

"Sold that watch yet, ole cobber?" I remarks.
    'E grabs 'is bag, an' views me battered dile,
With sudden fears uv spielers an' their larks.
    But I ixplain, an' 'e digs up a smile.
"Ah, yes," 'e drawls. "We met two nights ago
    But I was—well, you know—
        Well—jist so-so."

85

'E pipes me dile again, then stammers out,
    "I'm sorry, sonny. Stone the crows! It's sad
To see yer face so orful cut about.
    I never thort I walloped you so bad.
I'm sorry, lad, that we should come to blows.
    Black eye? An' wot a nose!
            Oh, stone the crows!

I ease 'is guilty mind about me phiz,
    An' we're good cobbers in a 'arf a tick.
Then 'e wades in an' tells me 'oo 'e is—
    ('E ain't a bad ole coot when 'e ain't shick)—
"I ain't dead broke," 'e sez. "That night, yeh know,
    I was cleaned out uv dough,
            An'—well—so-so."

Lookin' fer land 'e is; an' 'as 'is eye
    Upon a little farm jist close to me.
If 'e decides to take it by-an'-by,
    "Why, stone the crows! I'll look yous up," sez 'e.
"I need some friends: I ain't got wife nor chick;
    An' yous will like me quick—
            When I ain't shick."

I leaves 'im tork. Me own affairs won't let
    Me pay much 'eed to all 'e 'as to say.
But, while 'e's spoutin', sudden like I get
    A bright idear that brings one 'opeful ray.
One thing I 'eard pertickler while 'e spoke;
    'E is a single bloke.
            I lets that soak.

But later on I wished 'e'd sling 'is mag.
    The nearer 'ome I get the worse I feel;
The worse I feel, the more I chew the rag;
    The more I chew the rag, this crooked deal
I've served Doreen looks black an' blacker yet.
    I worry till I get
            All one cold sweat.

86

I walk 'ome frum the station, thinkin' 'ard.
  Wot can I tell me wife? Gawstruth! I been
Eight long years wed, an' never 'ad to guard
  Me tongue before. Wot can I tell Doreen?
An' there she's waitin' 'arf ways down our hill. . . .
    She takes one look . . . . "Why! Bill!"
              I stands stock still.

"Oh, yes, me face," I larfs. "O' course. Me face.
  I clean fergot. I—well—to tell the truth,
I—Don't look scared—I—Oh, it's no disgrace.
  That dentist. Yes, yes! Pullin' out me tooth.
Reel butcher. Nearly frachered both me jors.
    Yes, dear, lets go indoors."
              (Wow! 'Oly wars!)

Poor Bill! Poor Dear! 'E must 'ave been a brute."
  She kisses me fair on me busted lip;
An' all me fears is stilled be that serloot.
  Ar, wot a fool I was to 'ave the pip.
The game is mine before I 'ardly tried.
    Dead easy, 'ow I lied!
              I'm 'ome an' dried.

Yet. . . . I dunno. Me triump' don't last long.
  'Twuz low down, some way, 'ow I took 'er in—
Like pinchin' frum a kid. I feel dead wrong.
  The person calls it "conshusniss uv sin."
It might be; but it's got me worried now:
    An' conshuns is a cow,
              That I'll allow.

Take it frum me. To 'ave a lovin' wife
  Fussin' an' pettin' you, jist through a lie—
Like 'er this ev'nin'—crools all marrid life.
  If you can't look 'er fair bang in the eye
An' feel you've earned that trust frum first to last.
    You're 'eadin' downward fast. . . .
              But Rose—Oh, blast!

87

A WOMAN'S WAY

Women is strange. You take my tip; I'm wise.
  I know enough to know I'll never know
The 'uman female mind, or wot su'prise
  They 'as in store to bring yer boastin' low.
They keep yeh guessin' wot they're up to nex',
An' then, odds on, it's wot yeh least expecks.

Take me. I know me wife can twist me round
  'Er little finger. I don't mind that none.
Wot worries me is that I've never found
  Which way I'm gittin' twisted, till it's done.
Women is strange. An' yet, I've got to own
I'd make a orful 'ash uv it, alone.

There's this affair uv Rose. I tells yeh straight,
  Suspicious don't describe me state uv mind.
The calm way that Doreen 'as fixed the date
  An' all, looks like there's somethin' else be'ind.
Somethin'—not spite or meanness; don't think that.
Me wife purrs sometimes, but she ain't a cat.

But somethin'. I've got far too wise a nob
  To be took in by 'er airs uv repose.
I know I said I'd chuck the 'ole darn job
  An' leave 'er an' the parson deal with Rose.
But now me mind's uneasy, that's a fack.
I've got to manage things with speshul tack.

That's 'ow I feel—uneasy—when I drive
  Down to the train. I'm thinkin' as I goes,
There ain't two women, that I know, alive
  More dif'rint than them two—Doreen an' Rose.
'Ow they will mix together I dunno.
It all depends on 'ow I run the show.

Rose looks dead pale. She ain't got much to say
    ('Er few poor bits uv luggage make no load)
She smiles when we shake 'ands, an' sez Goodday
    Shy like an' strange; an' as we take the road
Back to the farm, I see 'er look around
Big-eyed, like it's some queer new land she's found.

I springs a joke or two. I'm none too bright
    Meself; but it's a slap-up sort uv day.
Spring's workin' overtime; to left an' right
    Blackwood an' wattle trees is bloomin' gay,
Blotchin' the bonzer green with golden dust;
An' magpies in 'em singin' fit to bust.

I sneak a glance at Rose. I can't look long.
    'Er lips is trem'lin'; tears is in 'er eye.
Then, glad with life, a thrush beefs out a song
    'Longside the road as we go drivin' by.
"Oh, Gawd A'mighty! 'Ark!" I 'ear 'er say,
"An' Spadgers Lane not fifty mile away!"

Not fifty mile away: the frowsy Lane,
    Where only dirt an' dreariness 'as sway,
Where every second tale's a tale uv pain,
    An' devil's doin's blots the night an' day.
But 'ere is thrushes tootin' songs uv praise.
An' golden blossoms lightin' up our ways.

I speaks a piece to boost this bonzer spot;
    Tellin' 'er 'ow the neighbour'ood 'as grown,
An' 'ow Dave Brown, jist up the road, 'as got
    Ten ton uv spuds per acre, usin' bone.
She don't seem to be list'nin'. She jist stares,
Like someone dreamin' dreams, or thinkin' pray'rs.

Me yap's a dud. No matter 'ow I try,
    Me conversation ain't the dinkum brand.
I'm 'opin' that she don't bust out an' cry:
    It makes me nervis. But I understand.
Over an' over I can 'ear 'er say,
"An' Spadgers less than fifty mile away!"

We're 'ome at last. Doreen is at the gate.
　I hitch the reins, an' quite the eager pup;
Then 'elp Rose down, an' stand aside an' wait
　To see 'ow them two size each other up.
But quick—like that—two arms 'as greeted warm
The sobbin' girl. . . . Doreen's run true to form.

"'Ome on the bit!" I thinks. But as I turn,
　'Ere's Wally Free 'as got to poke 'is dile
Above the fence, where 'e's been cuttin' fern.
　The missus spots 'im, an' I seen 'er smile.
An' then she calls to 'im: "Oh, Mister Free,
Come in," she sez, "an' 'ave a cup uv tea."

There's tack! A woman dunno wot it means.
　What does that blighter want with cups uv tea?
A privit, fambly meet—an' 'ere Doreen's
　Muckin' it all by draggin' in this Free.
She might 'ave knowed that Rose ain't feelin' prime,
An' don't want no strange comp'ny at the time.

Free an' 'is thievin' cow! But, all the same,
　'Is yap did seem to cheer Rose up a lot.
An' after, when 'e'd bunged 'is lanky frame
　Back to 'is job, Doreen sez, "Ain't you got
No work at all to do outside to-day?
Us two must 'ave a tork; so run away."

I went. . . . I went becoz, if I 'ad stayed,
　Me few remarks might 'ave been pretty 'ot.
Gawbli'me! 'Oo *is* 'ead uv this parade?
　Did I plan out the scheme, or did I not?
I've worked fer this, I've worried night an' day;
An' now it's fixed, I'm tole to "run away."

Women is strange. I s'pose I oughter be
　Contented; though I never un'erstands.
But when I score, it 'urts me dignerty
　To 'ave the credit grabbed out uv me 'ands.
I shouldn't look fer credit, p'raps; an' then,
Women is strange. But bli'me! So is men!

DIGGER SMITH

[*This book, like* Ginger Mick, *provides an example of the facility with which Dennis could follow up a success.* "Little Smith of Collingwood" *had gained only a passing reference earlier, but now (1918) he has become a central figure—type of the repatriated Digger and an interesting example of a city larrikin transplanted in the country. Six of thirteen tales in the book are given here.*]

DIGGER SMITH

'E CALLS me Digger; that's 'ow 'e begins.
'E sez 'e's only 'arf a man; an' grins.
  Judged be 'is nerve, I'd say 'e was worth two
              Uv me an' you.
Then 'e digs 'arf a fag out uv 'is vest,
Borrers me matches, an' I gives 'im best.

The first I 'eard about it Poole told me.
"There is a bloke called Smith at Flood's," sez 'e;
  Come there this mornin', sez 'e's come to stay,
              An' won't go 'way.
Sez 'e was sent there be a pal named Flood;
An' talks uv contracts sealed with Flanders mud.

"No matter wot they say, 'e only grins."
Sez Poole. "'E's rather wobbly on 'is pins.
  Seems like a soldier bloke. An' Peter Begg
              'E sez one leg
Works be machinery, but I dunno;
I only know 'e's there an' 'e won't go.

"'E grins," sez Poole, "at ev'rything they say.
Dad Flood 'as nearly 'ad a fit to-day.
  'E's cursed, an' ordered 'im clean off the place;
              But this cove's face
Jist goes on grinnin', an' 'e sez, quite carm,
'E's come to do a bit around the farm."

The tale don't sound too good to me at all.
"If 'e's a crook," I sez, "'e wants a fall.
  Maybe 'e's dilly. I'll go down an' see.
              'E'll grin at me
When I 'ave done, if 'e needs dealin' with."
So I goes down to interview this Smith.

'E 'ad a fork out in the tater patch.
Sez 'e, "Why, 'ello, Digger. Got a match?"
  "Digger?" I sez. "Well, you ain't digger 'ere.
            You better clear.
You ought to know that you can't dig them spuds.
They don't belong to you; they're ole Dad Flood's."

"Can't I?" 'e grins. "I'll do the best I can,
Considerin' I'm only 'arf a man.
  Give us a light. I can't get none from Flood,
            An' mine is dud."
I parts; an' 'e stands grinnin' at me still;
An' then 'e sez, "'Ave yeh fergot me, Bill?"

I looks, an' seen a tough bloke, short an' thin.
Then, Lord! I recomembers that ole grin.
  "It's little Smith!" I 'owls, "uv Collin'wood.
            Lad, this is good!
Last time I seen yeh, you an' Ginger Mick
Was 'owling rags, out on yer final kick."

"Yer on to it," 'e sez. "Nex' day we sailed.
Now 'arf uv me's back 'ome, an' 'arf they nailed
  An' Mick. . . . Ar, well, Fritz took me down a peg."
            'E waves 'is leg.
"It ain't too bad," 'e sez, with 'is ole smile;
"But when I starts to dig it cramps me style.

"But I ain't grouchin'. It was worth the fun.
We 'ad some picnic stoushin' Brother 'Un—
  The only fight I've 'ad that some John 'Op
            Don't come an' stop.
They pulled me leg a treat, but, all the same,
There's nothin' over 'ere to beat the game.

"An' now," 'e sez, "I'm 'ere to do a job
I promised, if it was me luck to lob
  Back 'ome before me mate," 'e sez, an' then,
            'E grins again.
"As clear as mud," I sez. "But I can't work
Me brains to 'old yer pace. Say, wot's the lurk?"

So then 'e puts me wise. It seems that 'im
An' this 'ere Flood—I tips it must be Jim—
    Was cobbers up in France, an' things occurred.
                (I got 'is word
Things did occur up there). But, anyway,
Seems Flood done somethin' good for 'im one day.

Then Smith 'e promised if 'e came back 'ome
Before 'is cobber o'er the flamin' foam,
    'E'd see the ole folks 'ere, an' 'e agreed,
                If there was need,
'E'd stay an' do a bit around the farm
So long as 'e 'ad one sound, dinkum arm.

"So, 'ere I am," 'e sez, an' grins again.
"A promise is a promise 'mong us men."
    Sez I, "You come along up to the 'ouse,
                Ole Dad won't rouse
When once 'e's got yer strength, an' as for Mar,
She'll kiss yeh when she finds out 'oo yeh are."

So we goes up, an' finds 'em both fair dazed
About this little Smith; they think 'e's crazed.
    I tells the tale in words they understand;
                Then it was grand
To see Dad grab Smith's 'and an' pump it good,
An' Mar, she kissed 'im, like I said she would.

Mar sez 'e must be starved, an' right away
The kettle's on, she's busy with a tray;
    An', when I left, this Digger Smith 'e looked
                Like 'e was booked
For keeps, with tea an' bread an' beef inside.
"Our little Willie's 'ome," 'e grins, 'an' dried!"

WEST

"I'VE seen so much uv dirt an' grime
  I'm mad to 'ave things clean.
I've seen so much uv death," 'e said—
"So many cobbers lyin' dead—
  You won't know wot I mean;
But, lad, I've 'ad so much uv strife
I want things straightened in my life.

"I've seen so much uv 'ate," 'e said—
  "Mad 'ate an' silly rage—
I'm yearnin' for clear thoughts," said 'e.
"Kindness an' love seem good to me.
  I want a new, white page
To start all over, clean an' good,
An' live me life as reel men should."

We're sittin' talkin' by the fence,
  The sun's jist goin' down,
Paintin' the sky all gold an' pink.
Said 'e. "When it's like that, I think—"
  An' then 'e stops to frown.
Said 'e, "I think, when it's jist so,
Uv . . . . God or somethin': I dunno.

"I ain't seen much uv God," said 'e;
  "Not 'ere nor Over There;
But, partly wot the padre said,
  It gits me when I stare
Out West when it's like that is now.
There must be somethin' else—some'ow.

"I've thought a lot," said Digger Smith—
  "Out There I thought a lot.
I thought uv death, an' all the rest,
An' uv me mates, good mates gone West;
  An' it ain't much I've got;
But things get movin' in me 'ead
When I look over there," 'e said.

"I've seen so much uv death," said 'e,
    "Me mind is in a whirl.
I've 'ad so many thoughts uv late." . . .
Said I, "Now, tell me, tell me straight,
    Own up; ain't there a girl?"
Said 'e, "I've done the best I can.
Wot does she want with 'arf a man?"

It weren't no use. 'E wouldn't talk
    Uv nothin' but the sky.
Said 'e. "Now, dinkum, talkin' square,
When you git gazin' over there
    Don't you 'arf want to cry?
I wouldn't be su'prised to see
An angel comin' out," said 'e.

The gold was creepin' up, the sun
    Was 'arf be'ind the range:
It don't seem strange a man should cry
To see that glory in the sky—
    To me it don't seem strange.
"Digger!" said 'e. "Look at it now!
There *must* be somethin' else—some'ow."

OVER THE FENCE

'Tain't my idea uv argument to call a man a fool,
An' I ain't lookin' round for bricks to 'eave at ole man Poole;
    But when 'e gets disputin' 'e's inclined to lose 'is 'ead.
    It ain't so much 'is choice uv words as 'ow the words is said.

'E's sich a coot for takin' sides, as I sez to Doreen.
Sez she, "'Ow can 'e, by 'imself?"—wotever that may mean.
    My wife sez little things sometimes that nearly git me riled.
    I knoo she meant more than she said be that soft way she smiled.

Today, when I was 'arrowin', Poole comes down to the fence
To get the loan uv my long spade; an' uses that pretence
    To 'ave a bit uv friendly talk, an' one word leads to more,
    As is the way with ole man Poole, as I've remarked before.

The spade reminds 'im 'ow 'e done some diggin' in 'is day,
An' diggin' brings the talk to earth, an' earth leads on to clay,
    Then clay quite natural reminds a thinkin' bloke uv bricks,
    An' mortar brings up mud, an' then, uv course, it's politics.

Now, Poole sticks be 'is Party, an' I don't deny 'is right;
But when 'e starts abusin' mine 'e's lookin' for a fight.
    So I delivers good 'ome truths about 'is crowd; then Poole
    Wags 'is ole beard across the fence an' tells me I'm a fool.

Now, that's the dizzy limit; so I lays aside the reins,
An' starts to prove 'e's storin' mud where most blokes keeps their
    brains.
    'E decorates 'is answers, an' we're goin' it ding-dong,
    When this returned Bloke, Digger Smith, comes saunterin' along.

Poole's gripped the fence as though 'e means to tear the rail in two,
An' eyes my waggin' finger like 'e wants to 'ave a chew.
    Then Digger Smith 'e grins at Poole, an' then 'e looks at me,
    An' sez, quite soft an' friendly-like, "Winnin' the war?" sez 'e.

Now, Poole deserves it, an' I'm pleased the lad give 'im that jolt.
'E goes fair mad in argument when once 'e gets a holt.
   "Yeh make me sad," sez Digger Smith; "the both uv you," sez 'e.
   "The both uv us! Gawstruth!" sez I. "You ain't includin' me?"

"Well, it takes two to make a row," sez little Digger Smith.
"A bloke can't argue 'less 'e 'as a bloke to argue with
   I've come 'ome from a dinkum scrap to find this land uv light
   Is chasin' its own tail around an' callin' it a fight.

"We've seen a thing or two, us blokes 'oo've fought on many fronts;
An' we've 'ad time to think a bit between the fightin' stunts.
   We've seen big things, an' thought big things, an' all the silly fuss,
   That used to get us rattled once, seems very small to us.

"P'r'aps we 'ave 'ad some skite knocked out, an p'r'aps we see more
      clear,
But seems to us there's plenty cleanin'-up to do round 'ere.
   We've learnt a little thing or two, an' we 'ave unlearnt 'eaps,
   An' silly partisans, with us, is counted out for keeps.

"This takin' sides jist for the sake uv takin' sides—Aw, 'Struth!
I used to do them things one time, back in me foolish youth.
   Out There, when I remembered things, I've kicked meself reel
      good.
   In football days I barracked once red 'ot for Collin'wood.

"I didn't want to see a game, nor see no justice done.
It never mattered wot occurred as long as my side won;
   The other side was narks an' cows an' rotters to a man,
   But mine was all reel bonzer chaps. I was a partisan.

"It might sound like swelled-'ead," sez Smith. "But show me, if yeh
      can." . . .
" 'Old 'ard," sez Poole. "Jist tell me this: wot is a partisan?"
   Then Digger Smith starts to ixplain; Poole interrupts straight out;
   An' I wades in to give my views, an' 'as to nearly shout.

We battles on for one good hour. My team sleeps where it stands;
An' Poole 'as tossed the spade away to talk with both 'is 'ands;
   An' Smith 'as dropped the maul 'e 'ad. Then I looks round to see
   Doreen quite close. She smiles at us. "Winnin' the war?" sez she.

A DIGGER'S TALE

" 'My oath!" the Duchess sez. 'You'd not ixpect
   Sich things as that. Yeh don't mean kangaroos?
Go hon!' she sez, or words to that effect—
   (It's 'ard to imitate the speech they use)—
I tells 'er, 'Straight; I drives 'em four-in-'and
      'Ome in my land.'

"You 'ear a lot," sez little Digger Smith,
   "About 'ow English swells is so stand-off.
Don't yeh believe it; it's a silly myth.
   I've been reel cobbers with the British toff
While I'm on leave; for Blighty liked our crowd,
      An' done us proud.

"Us Aussies was the goods in London town
   When I was there. If they jist twigged yer 'at
The Dooks would ask yeh could yeh keep one down,
   An' Earls would 'ang out 'Welcome' on the mat
An' sling yeh invites to their stately 'alls
      For fancy balls.

"This Duchess—I ain't quite sure uv 'er rank;
   She might uv been a Peeress. I dunno.
I meets 'er 'usband first. 'E owns a bank,
   I 'eard, an' 'arf a dozen mints or so.
A dinkum toff. 'E sez, 'Come 'ome with me
      An' 'ave some tea.'

"That's 'ow I met this Duchess Wot's-er-name—
   Or Countess—never mind 'er moniker;
I ain't no 'and at this 'ere title game—
   An' right away, I was reel pals with 'er.
'Now, tell me all about yer 'ome,' sez she,
      An' smiles at me.

"That knocks me out. I know it ain't no good
  Paintin' word-picters uv the things I done
Out 'ome 'ere, barrackin' for Collin'wood,
  Or puntin' on the flat at Flemington.
I know this Baroness uv Wot-yeh-call
        Wants somethin' tall.

"I thinks reel 'ard; an' then I lets it go.
  I tells 'er, out at Richmond, on me Run—
A little place uv ten square mile or so—
  I'm breedin' boomerangs; which is reel fun,
When I ain't troubled by the wild Jonops
        That eats me crops.

"I talks about the wondrous Boshter Bird
  That builds 'er nest up in the Cobber Tree,
An' 'atches out 'er young on May the third,
  Stric' to the minute, jist at 'arf pas' three.
'Er eyes get big. She sez, 'Can it be true?'
        'Er eyes was blue.

"An' then I speaks uv sport, an' tells 'er 'ow
  In 'untin' our wild Wowsers we imploy
Large packs uv Barrackers, an' 'ow their row
  Wakes echoes in the forests uv Fitzroy,
Where lurks the deadly Shicker Snake 'oo's breath
        Is certain death.

"I'm goin' on to talk uv kangaroos,
  An' 'ow I used to drive 'em four-in-'and.
'Wot?' sez the Marchioness. 'Them things in Zoos
  That 'ops about? I've seen 'em in the Strand
In *double 'arness*; but I ain't seen four.
        Tell me some more.'

"I baulks a bit at that; an' she sez, 'Well,
  There ain't no cause at all for you to feel
Modest about the things you 'ave to tell;
  An' wot yeh say sounds wonderfully reel.
Your talk'—an' 'ere I seen 'er eyelids flick—
        'Makes me 'omesick.

" 'I reckerlect,' she sez—'Now, let me see—
    In Gippsland, long ago, when I was young,
I 'ad a little pet Corroboree'
    (I sits up in me chair like I was stung);
'On its 'ind legs,' she sez, 'it used to stand.
            Fed from me 'and.'

"Uv course, I threw me alley in right there.
    This Princess was a dinkum Aussie girl.
I can't do nothin' else but sit an' stare,
    Thinkin' so rapid that me 'air roots curl.
But 'er? She sez, 'I ain't 'eard talk so good
            Since my child'ood.

" 'I wish,' sez she, 'I could be back again
    Beneath the wattle an' that great blue sky.
It's like a breath uv 'ome to meet you men.
    You've done reel well,' she sez. 'Don't you be shy.
When yer in Blighty once again,' sez she,
            'Come an' see me.

"I don't see 'er no more; 'cos I stopped one.
    But, 'fore I sails, I gits a billy doo
Which sez, 'Give my love to the dear ole Sun,
    An' take an exile's blessin' 'ome with you.
An' if you 'ave some boomerangs to spare,
            Save me a pair.

" 'I'd like to see 'em play about,' she wrote,
    'Out on me lawn, an' stroke their pretty fur.
God bless yeh, boy.' An' then she ends 'er note,
    'Yer dinkum cobber,' an' 'er moniker.
A sport? You bet! She's marri'd to an Earl—
            An Aussie girl."

HALF A MAN

"I wash me 'ands uv 'im," I tells 'em, straight.
　"You women can do wot yeh dash well like
I leave this 'arf a man to 'is own fate;
　I've done me bit, an' now I'm gone on strike.
Do wot yeh please; but don't arsk 'elp from me;
'E's give me nerves; so now I'll let 'im be."

Doreen an' ole Mar Flood 'as got a scheme.
　They've been conspirin' for a week or more
About this Digger Smith, an' now they dream
　They've got 'is fucher waitin' in cool store
To 'and 'im out, an' fix 'im up for life.
But they've got Buckley's, as I tells me wife.

I've seen 'em whisperin' up in our room.
　Now they wants me to join in the debate;
But, "Nix," I tells 'em. "I ain't in the boom,
　An' Digger Smith ain't risin' to me bait;
'E's fur too fly a fish for me to catch,
An' two designin' women ain't 'is match."

I puts me foot down firm, an' tells 'em, No!
　Their silly plan's a thing I wouldn't touch.
An' then me wife, for 'arf an hour or so,
　Talks to me confident, of nothin' much;
Then, 'fore I know it, I am all red 'ot
Into the scheme, an' leader uv the plot.

'Twas Mar Flood starts it. She got 'old uv 'im—
　You know the way they 'ave with poor, weak **men**—
She drops a tear or two concernin' Jim;
　Tells 'im wot women 'ave to bear; an' then
　She got 'im talkin', like a woman can.
'E never would 'ave squeaked to any man.

She leads 'im on—it's crook the way they scheme—
    To talk about this girl 'e's left be'ind.
Not that she's pryin'! Why, she wouldn't dream!—
    But speakin' uv it might jist ease 'is mind.
Then, 'fore 'e knows, 'e's told, to 'is su'prise,
Name an' address—an' colour uv 'er eyes!

An' then she's off 'ere, plottin' with Doreen—
    Bustin' a confidence, I tells 'em, flat.
But all me roustin' leaves 'em both serene:
    Women don't see a little thing like that.
An' I ain't cooled off yet before they've got
Me workin' for 'em in this crooked plot.

Nex' day Mar Flood she takes 'er Sund'y dress
    An' 'er best little bonnet up to town.
'Er game's to see the girl at this address
    An' sprag 'er in regard to comin' down
To take Smith be su'prise. My part's to fix
A meetin' so there won't be any mix.

I tips, some'ow, that girl won't 'esitate.
    She don't. She comes right back with Mar nex' day,
All uv a fluster. When I seen 'er state
    I thinks I'd best see Digger straight away;
'Cos, if I don't, 'e's bound to 'ear the row,
With 'er: "Where is 'e? Can't I see 'im now?"

I finds 'im in the paddick down at Flood's.
    I 'ums an' 'ars a bit about the crops.
'E don't say nothin': goes on baggin' spuds.
    "'Ow would yeh like?" I sez to 'im, an' stops.
"'Ow would it be?" . . . 'E stands an' looks at me:
"Now, wot the 'Ell's got into you?" sez 'e.

That don't restore me confidence a bit—
    The drarmer isn't goin' as I tipped.
I corfs, an' makes another shot at it,
    While 'e looks at me like 'e thinks I'm dipped.
"Well—jist suppose?" I sez; an' then I turn
An' see 'er standin' there among the fern.

104

She don't want no prelimin'ries, this tart;
  She's broke away before they rung the bell;
She's beat the gun, an' got a flyin' start.
  Smith makes a funny noise, an' I sez, "'Ell!"
An' gives 'em imitations uv the chase.
But, as I went, I caught sight uv 'er face.

That's all I want to know. An', as I ran,
  I 'ears 'er cry, "My man! Man an' a 'arf!
Don't fool me with yer talk uv 'arf a man!" . . . .
  An' then I 'ears ole Digger start to larf.
It was a funny larf, so 'elp me bob:
Fair in the middle uv it come a sob . . . .

I don't see Digger till the other night.
  "Well, 'Arf-a-man," I sez. " 'Ow goes it now?"
"Yes, 'arf a man," sez 'e. "Yeh got it right;
  I can't change that, alone, not any'ow.
But she is mendin' things." 'E starts to larf.
"Some day," 'e sez, "she'll be the better 'arf."

JIM

"Now, be the Hokey Fly!" sez Peter Begg.
"Suppose 'e comes 'ome with a wooden leg.
   Suppose 'e isn't fit to darnce at all,
    Then, ain't we 'asty fixin' up this ball?
A little tournament at Bridge is my
Idear," sez Peter. "Be the Hokey Fly!"

Ole Peter Begg is gettin' on in years.
'E owns a reel good farm; an' all 'e fears
   Is that some girl will land 'im, by an' by,
    An' share it with 'im—be the Hokey Fly.
That's 'is pet swear-word, an' I dunno wot
'E's meanin', but 'e uses it a lot.

"Darncin'!" growls Begg. We're fixin' up the 'all
With bits uv green stuff for a little ball
   To welcome Jim, 'oo's comin' 'ome nex' day.
    We're 'angin' flags around to make things gay,
An' shiftin' chairs, an' candle-greasin' floors,
As is our way when blokes come 'ome from wars.

"A little game uv Bridge," sez Peter Begg,
"Would be more decent like, an' p'r'aps a keg
   Uv somethin' if the 'ero's feelin' dry.
    But this 'ere darncin'! Be the Hokey Fly,
These selfish women never thinks at all
About the guest; they only wants the ball.

"Now, cards," sez Begg, "amuses ev'ry one.
An' then our soldier guest could 'ave 'is fun
   If 'ed lost *both* 'is legs. It makes me sick—
    'Ere! Don't yeh spread that candle-grease too thick.
Yeh're wastin' it; an' us men 'as to buy
Enough for nonsense, be the Hokey Fly!"

Begg, 'e ain't never keen on wastin' much.
"Peter," I sez, "it's you that needs a crutch.
    Why don't yeh get a wife, an' settle down?"
    'E looks reel fierce, an' answers, with a frown,
"Do you think I am goin' to be rooked
For 'arf me tucker, jist to get it cooked?"

I lets it go at that, an' does me job;
An' when a little later on I lob
    Along the 'omeward track, down by Flood's gate
    I meet ole Digger Smith, an' stops to state
Me views about the weather an' the war . . . .
'E tells me Jim gets 'ere nex' day, at four.

An', as we talk, I sees along the road
A strange bloke 'umpin' some queer sort uv load.
    I points 'im out to Smith an' sez, " 'Oo's that?
    Looks like a soldier, don't 'e, be 'is 'at?"
"Stranger," sez Digger, "be the cut uv 'im."
But, trust a mother's eyes. . . . *"It's Jim! My Jim!*

"My Jim!" I 'ears; an', scootin' up the track
Come Missus Flood, with Flo close at 'er back.
    It was a race, for lover an' for son;
    They finished neck an' neck; but mother won,
For it was 'er that got the first good 'ug.
(I'm so took back I stands there like a mug.)

Then come Flo's turn; an' Jim an' Digger they
Shake 'ands without no fancy, gran'-stand play.
    Yeh'd think they parted yesterd'y, them two,
    For all the wild 'eroics that they do.
"Yeh done it, lad," sez Jim. "I knoo yeh would."
"You bet," sez Smith; "but I'm all to the good."

Then, uv a sudden, all their tongues is loosed.
They finds me there an' I am intrajuiced;
    An' Jim tells 'ow it was 'e come to land
    So soon, while Mar an' Flo each 'olds a 'and.
But, jist as sudden, they all stop an' stare
Down to the 'ouse, at Dad Flood standin' there.

I

'E's got 'is 'and up shadin' off the sun.
Then 'e starts up to them; but Dad don't run:
    'E isn't 'owlin' for 'is lost boy's kiss;
    'E's got 'is own sweet way in things like this.
'E wanders up, an' stands an' looks at Jim;
An', spare me days, that look was extra grim!

I seen the mother pluckin' at 'er dress;
I seen the girl's white face an' 'er distress.
    An' Digger Smith, 'e looks reel queer to me:
    Grinnin' inside 'imself 'e seemed to be.
At last Dad sez—oh, 'e's a tough ole gun!—
"Well, are yeh sorry now for wot yeh done?"

Jim gives a start; but answers with a grin,
"Well, Dad, I 'ave been learnin' discipline.
    An' tho' I ain't quite sure wot did occur
    Way back"—'e's grinnin' worse—"I'm sorry, sir."
(It beats me, that, about these soldier blokes:
They're always grinnin', like all things was jokes.)

P'r'aps Dad is gettin' dull in 'is ole age;
But 'e don't seem to see Jim's cammyflage.
    P'r'aps 'e don't want to; for, in 'is ole eye,
    I seen a twinkle as 'e give reply.
"Nex' week," 'e sez, "we will begin to cart
The taters. Yeh can make another start."

But then 'e grabs Jim's 'and. I seen the joy
In mother's eyes. "Now, welcome 'ome, me boy,"
    Sez Dad; an' then 'e adds, "Yeh've made me proud;'
    That's all. An' 'e don't say it none too loud.
Dad don't express 'is feelin's in a shout;
It cost 'im somethin' to git that much out.

      .   .   .   .   .   .

We 'ad the darnce. An', spite uv all Begg's fears,
Jim darnced like 'e could keep it up for years;
    Mostly with Flo. We don't let up till three;
    An' then ole Peter Begg, Doreen an' me
We walk together 'ome, an' on the way,
Doreen 'as quite a lot uv things to say.

"Did you see Flo?" sez she. "Don't she look grand?
That Jim's the luckiest in all the land—
   An' little Smith—that girl uv 'is, I'm sure,
   She'll bring 'im 'appiness that will endure."
She 'ugs my arm, then sez, " 'Usband or wife,
If it's the right one, is the wealth uv life."

I sneaks a look at Begg, an' answers, "Yes,
Yeh're right, ole girl; that's the reel 'appiness.
   An' if ole, lonely growlers was to know
   The worth uv 'appy marridge 'ere below,
They'd swap their bank-books for a wife," sez I.
Sez Peter Begg, *"Well! Be the—Hokey—Fly!"*

JIM OF THE HILLS

[The story of Jim, published in 1919, records
in some measure its author's reaction to the
world about him at "Toolangi on the rise"—the
birds, the trees, the work of timbermen, and the
menace of forest fires. This time he left behind
the slang of city lanes, using instead more or less
"straight" English with merely a dropped letter
here and there. Six of twelve poems are quoted.]

A MORNING SONG

THE thrush is in the wattle tree, an', "O, you pretty dear!"
He's callin' to his little wife for all the bush to hear.
   He's wantin' all the bush to know about his charmin' hen;
   He sings it over fifty times, an' then begins again.
For it's Mornin'! Mornin'! The world is wet with dew,
With tiny drops a-twinkle where the sun comes shinin' thro'.

The thrush is in the wattle tree, red robin's underneath,
The little blue-cap's dodgin' in an' out amongst the heath;
   An' they're singin', boy, they're singin' like they'd bust 'emselves
      to bits;
   While, up above, old Laughin' Jack is havin' forty fits.
For it's Mornin'! Mornin'! The leaves are all ashine:
There's treasure all about the place; an' all of it is mine.

Oh, it's good to be a wealthy man, it's grand to be a king
With mornin' on the forest-land an' joy in everything.
   It's fine to be a healthy man with healthy work to do
   In the singin' land, the clean land, washed again with dew.
When sunlight slants across the trees, an' birds begin to sing,
Then kings may snore in palaces, but I'm awake—and king.

But the king must cook his breakfast, an' the king must sweep the
      floor;
Then out with axe on shoulder to his kingdom at the door,
   His old dog sportin' on ahead, his troubles all behind,
   An' joy mixed in the blood of him because the world is kind.
For it's Mornin'! Mornin'! Time to out an' strive!
Oh, there's not a thing I'm askin' else but just to be alive!

My friends are in the underbrush, my friends are in the trees,
An' merrily they welcome me with mornin' melodies.
   Above, below, from bush an' bough each calls his tuneful part;
   An' best of all, one trusty friend is callin' in my heart.
For it's Mornin'! Mornin'! When night's black troubles end.
An' never man was friendless yet who stayed his own good friend.

Grey thrush is in the wattle, an' it's, "O, you pretty dear!"
He's callin' to his little wife, an' don't care who should hear
    In the great bush, the fresh bush, washed again with dew;
    An' my axe is on my shoulder, an' there's work ahead to do.
Oh, it's Mornin'! Singin' Mornin'! in the land I count the best,
An' with the heart an' mind of me I'm singin' with the rest.

THE VISION

Of things that roam about the bush I ain't got many fears,
For I knows their ways an' habits, an' I've chummed with them for
    years.
  For man or beast or gully ghost I've pluck enough to spare;
  But I draws the line at visions with the sunlight in their hair.

I was feelin' fine this mornin' when I started out to work;
An' I caught myself high-steppin' with a boastful sort of jerk;
  With my head a trifle higher an' my eye a little stern.
  I thought the world was mine for keeps; but I'd a lot to learn.

I was workin' at the rip saw; for the boss had called me in
From the peaceful bush an' quiet to the sawmill's fuss an' din;
  An' there he put me tailin' out—a game I never like;
  But, "Likin' isn't gettin' in the bush," says Daddy Pike.

I was workin' at the rip saw, cursin' at my achin' back,
When I saw the blessed vision comin' down the log-yard track.
  There were others in the party, but the one that got my stare
  Was her with two brown, laughin' eyes an' sunlight in her hair.

"More visitors!" growled old man Pike. "Another city push.
I'll bet a quid they ask us why we 'spoil the lovely bush'."
  I hardly heard him saying it, for like a fool I stand,
  My eyes full of the vision an' a batten in my hand.

"You gone to sleep?" the sawyer said. "What's got you mesmerized?"
I start to work like fury, but my thoughts can't be disguised.
  "Oh, Jim's gone dippy with the Spring," replies old Pike an' grins.
  I turn to answer dignified; but trip, an' bark my shins.

Next thing I know the boss is there, an' talkin' fine an' good,
Explainin' to the visitors how trees are made of wood.
  They murmur things like "Marvellous!" an' "What a monster
    tree!"
  An' then the one with sunlit hair comes right bang up to me.

"I saw you fall," she sort of sung: you couldn't say she talked,
For her voice had springtime in it, like the way she looked an'
    walked.
  "I saw you fall," she sung at me. "I hope you were not hurt?"
  An' suddenly I was aware I wore my oldest shirt.

"It never hurt me half as much as your two smilin' eyes."
That's how I could have answered her—an' watched old Pike's
    surprise—
  "It never harmed me half as much as standin' here like this
  With tattered shirt an' grimy hands" . . . But I just says, "No,
    Miss."

"Oh, no," I says. "We're pretty hard, an' have to take them cracks."
(But, just to see her sudden smile, made me as soft as wax.)
  "You're strong," she smiles. I answers, "Oh, I'm pretty strong, all
    right."
  An' close behind I heard old Pike observin', "Hear 'im skite!"

That finished me. I lost what little nerve I had, an' grew
Dead certain that I looked a fool, an' that she thought so, too.
  She talked some more; but I can't tell what other things she said—
  I went all cold, except my ears, an' they were burnin' red.

I only know her eyes were soft, her voice was kind an' low.
I never spoke another word exceptin' "Yes" an' "No".
  I never felt a bigger chump in all my livin' days,
  Well knowin' I was gettin' worse at every word she says.

An' when the knock-off whistle blew, Ben Murray he came by,
An' says he'd like a private talk; but, "Pickle it," says I.
  " 'Twill have to keep till later on." He answers, "As you like."
  Soon after that I saw him talkin' earnest with old Pike.

If I'd been right, I might have known there's somethin' in the air
By the way the blokes were actin'; but a fat lot did I care.
  Swell visions an' the deadly pip was what was wrong with me.
  I slung a word to my old dog, an' we trudged home to tea.

An' after, in the same old way, we sits beside the fire,
To have a talk, my dog an' me, on fools an' vain desire.
  I tell him I'm a silly chump to think the things I do;
  An', with a waggle of his tail, he says he thinks so too.

I tell him I suppose she's rich, or so she seems to be;
Most likely some reel city swell—an' he don't disagree.
  I says to him the chances are I'll not see her no more.
  Then he gives me a funny look, an' curls up on the floor.

But I was slow to take the tip, an' went on talkin' rot
About injustice in the world, an' boiled up good an' hot.
  I spouts of wrongs of workin' men an' how our rulers fail.
  His eyes are shut, but he just seconds motions with his tail.

All beauty's only for the rich, all times, an' every way.
The toilers just take what is left, as I've heard Murray say
  When he's been talkin' to the boys about the workers' rights,
  An' spoutin' of equality, down at the huts, of nights.

I turned the social system inside-out for my old dog,
Tho' he don't seem much entertained, but lies there like a log.
  I spoke of common people's wrongs—especially of mine;
  But when I came to mention love I thought I heard him whine.

But I went on, an' said straight out that, tho' I seemed above
Such nonsense once, I'd changed a bit, an' I believed in love.
  I said love was a splendid thing! . . . Then, true as I am born,
  He rose, an' yawned, an' shut me up with one crook glance of
    scorn.

It's bad enough to be a bloke without one reel close friend;
But when your dog gives you the bird it's pretty near the end.
  Ashamed, I sneaked away to bunk; an' fell to dreamin' there
  Of a little brown-eyed vision with the sunlight in her hair.

THE WOOER

I NEARLY fell fair in my tracks.
I'm trudgin' homeward with my axe
    When I come on her suddenly.
    "I wonder if I'm lost?" says she.
"It's risky on such roads as this."
I lifts my hat an' says, "Yes, miss."
    I knew 'twas rude for me to stare,
    But, oh, that sunlight in her hair!

"I wonder if I'm lost?" says she,
An' gives a smile that staggers me.
    "An' yet, it wouldn't matter much
    Supposing that I was, with such
A glorious green world about,
With bits of blue sky peepin' out.
    Do *you* think there will be a fog?"
    "No, miss," says I, an' pats my dog.

"Oh, what a dear old dog!" says she.
"Most dogs are pretty fond of me."
    She calls him to her, an' he goes.
    (He didn't find it hard, I s'pose;
I know I wouldn't, if she called.)
"It's wondrous how the tracks are walled
    With these great trees that touch the sky
    On either side." "Yes, miss," says I.

She fondles my old dog a bit;
I wait to make a bolt for it.
    (There ain't no call to stand an' talk
    With one who'd be too proud to walk
A half-a-yard with such as me.)
"The wind seems workin' up," says she.
    "Yes, miss," I says, an' lifts me hat.
    An' she just lets it go at that.

118

She lets me reach the dribblin' ford—
That day to me it fairly roared.
   (At least, that's how the thing appears;
   But blood was poundin' in my ears.)
She waits till I have fairly crossed:
"I thought I told you I was lost?"
   She cries. "An' you go walkin' off,
   Quite scornful, like some proud bush toff!"

She got me thinkin' hard with that.
"Yes, miss," I says, an' lifts my hat.
   But she just waits there on the track,
   An' lets me walk the whole way back.
"An' are you reely lost?" says I.
"Yes, sir," says she, an' drops her eye . . .
   I wait, an' wait for what seems days;
   But not another word she says.

I pats my dog, an' lifts my hat;
But she don't seem to notice that.
   I looks up trees an' stares at logs,
   An' long for twenty hats an' dogs.
"The weather's kept reel good to-day,"
I blurts at last. Says she, "Hurray!"
   "Hurray!" she says, an' then, "Encore!"
   An' gets me wonderin' what for.

"Is this the right road to 'The Height'?"
I tell her it's the road, all right,
   But that the way she's walkin' ain't.
   At that she looked like she would faint.
"Then I *was* lost if I had gone
Along this road an' walked right on—
   An unfrequented bush track, too!
   How fortunate that I met you!"

"Yes, miss," I says. "Yes—what?" says she.
Says I, "Most fortunate . . . for me."
   I don't know where I found the pluck
   To blurt that out an' chance my luck.

"You'll walk," she says, "a short way back,
So you can put me on the track?"
  "I'll take you *all* the way," says I,
  An' looks her fair bang in the eye.

Later, I let myself right out,
An' talked; an' told her all about
  The things I've done, an' what I do,
  An' nearly all I'm hopin' to.
Told why I chose the game I'm at
Because my folks were poor, an' that.
  She seemed reel pleased to hear me talk,
  An' sort of steadied up the walk.

An' when I'd spoke my little bit,
She just takes up the thread of it;
  An' later on, near knocks me down
  By tellin' me she *works*—in town.
Works? Her? I thought, the way she dressed,
She was quite rich; but she confessed
  That makin' dresses was her game,
  An' she was dead sick of the same.

When Good-bye came, I lifts my hat;
But she holds out her hand at that.
  I looked at mine, all stained with sap,
  An' told her I'm a reel rough chap.
"A worker's hand," says she, reel fine,
"An' marked with toil; but so is mine.
  We're just two toilers; let us shake,
  An' be good friends—for labour's sake."

At home I looks around the place,
An' sees the dirt's a fair disgrace;
  So takes an' tidies up a bit,
  An' has a shave; an' then I sit
Beside my fire to have a think.   .
But my old dog won't sleep a wink;
  He fools, an' whines, an' nudges me,
  Then all at once I thinks of tea.

I beg his pardon with a smile,
An', talkin' to him all the while,
    I get it ready, tellin' him
    About that girl; but, "Shut up, Jim!"
He says to me as plain as plain.
"First have some food, an' then explain."
    (I don't know how she came to tell,
    But I found out her name is Nell.)

We gets our bit to eat at last
(An', just for spite, he et his fast) . . .
    I think that Nell's a reel nice name . .
    "All right, old dog, I ain't to blame
If you" . . . Just as I go to sup
My tea I stop dead, with my cup
    Half up, an' . . . By the Holy Frost!
    I wonder was Nell reely lost?

RED ROBIN

Hi, it's a funny world! This mornin', when I woke
I saw red robin on the fence, an' heard the words he spoke.
  Red robin, he's a perky chap, an' this was his refrain:
  "Dear, it's a pity that poor Jenny is so plain."

To talk like that about his wife! It had me scandalized.
I'd heard him singin' so before, but never recognized
  The meaning of his chatter, or that he could be so vain:
  "Dear, it's a pity that poor Jenny is so plain."

I don't know how, I don't know why, but this reminded me
I was promised to the widow for this Sunday night to tea.
  I'd promised her for weeks an' weeks, until she pinned me down.
  I recollects this is the day, an' gets up with a frown.

I was thinkin' of the widow while I gets me clobber on—
Like a feller will start thinkin' of the times that's past an' gone.
  An', while my thoughts is runnin' so, that bird chips in again:
  "Dear, it's a pity that poor Jenny is so plain."

Now, the widow's name is Jenny, an' it strikes me sort of queer
That my thoughts should be upon her when that robin's song I hear.
  She ain't so homely neither; but she never could compare
  With a certain bonzer vision with the sunlight in her hair.

When I wander down that evenin', she come smilin' to the gate,
An' her look is calculatin', as she scolds because I'm late.
  She takes my hat an' sits me down an' heaves a little sigh
  But I get a queer sensation from that glimmer in her eye.

She starts to talk about the mill, an' then about the strike,
An' then she digs Ben Murray up an' treats him nasty-like;
  She treats him crool an' cattish, as them soft, sweet women can,
  But I ups an' tells her plainly that I think Ben is a man.

First round to me. But she comes back, an' says Ben is a cad
Who's made a laughin'-stock of her, an' treated her reel bad.
  I twig she's out for sympathy; so counters that, an' says
  That Ben's a broken-hearted man about the mill these days.

The second round to me on points; an' I was havin' hopes.
(I might have known that widows were familiar with the ropes.)
  "But he'd *never* make a husband!" says the widow, with a sigh.
  An' again I gets a warnin' from that glimmer in her eye.

I says I ain't no judge of that; an' treats it with a laugh.
But she keeps the talk on husbands for a minute an' a half.
  I can't do much but spar a bit, an' keep her out of range;
  So the third round is the widow's; an' the fight takes on a change.

I'm longin' for a breather, for I've done my nerve a lot,
When suddenly she starts on "Love", an' makes the pace reel hot.
  In half a jiff she has me on the ropes, an' breathin' hard,
  With not a fight inside me—I can only duck an' guard.

She uppercuts me with a sigh, an' jabs me with a glance.
(When a widow is the fighter, has a single bloke a chance?)
  Her short-arm blows are amorous, most lovin' is her lunge;
  Until it's just a touch an' go I don't throw up the sponge.

I use my head-piece here a bit to wriggle from the fix;
For the widow is a winner 'less I fluke a win by tricks.
  An' I gets a reel mean notion (that I don't seek to excuse),
  When I interrupts her rudely with, "But have you heard the
    news?"

Now, to a woman, that's a lead dead certain of a score,
An' a question that the keenest is unable to ignore.
  An' good old Curiosity comes in to second me,
  As I saw her struggle hopeless, an' "What news is that?" says she.

An' here I spins a lovely yarn, a gloomy, hard-luck tale
Of how I've done my money in, an' I'm about to fail,
  How my house an' land is mortgaged, how I've muddled my affairs
  Through foolin' round with racin' bets an' rotten minin' shares.

I saw the fight was easy mine the minute I begun;
An', after half a dozen words, the time-keep counted "one".
    An' when I finish that sad tale there ain't the slightest doubt
    I am the winner of the contest, an' the widow's down an' out.

But not for long. Although she's lost, the widow is dead game:
"I'm sorry, Mister Jim," says she, "for both your loss an' shame.
    All things is changed between us now, of course; the past is dead.
    An' what you were about to say you please will leave unsaid."

    .   .   .   .

I was thinkin' in the evenin' over how I had escaped,
An' how the widow took it all—the way she stared an' gaped.
    She looked her plainest at that time; but that don't matter now;
    For, plain, or fair, I know of one who's fairer, anyhow.

I tells meself that beauty ain't a thing to count with man,
An' I would never choose a wife on that unthinkin' plan.
    No robin was awake, I swear; but still I heard that strain:
    "Dear, it's a pity that poor Jenny is so plain."

FLAMES

It's human nature for a bashful bloke
  To bottle up, an' hesitate, an' doubt
Till grinnin' Fate plays him some low-down joke;
  Then, in excitement, he goes blurtin' out
The tale his sane mind never would impart,
So all the near-by world knows it by heart.

Good luck for me, the near-by world that day,
  When I ran sobbin' thro' the scorchin' fern,
Held few to hear the foolish things I say:
  No one was there my secret thought to learn,
As I went shoutin' down the mountain spur,
Only the scared birds, an' the trees, an' Her.

In fancy, many men have been thro' Hell,
  Tortured by fear, when hope has almost died;
But few have gone thro' that, an' fire as well
  To come on Heaven at the other side
With just one angel in it, safe an' well—
A cool, calm angel by the name of Nell.

The day the fire came sweepin' down the hill,
  Lickin' the forest up like some mad beast,
We had our work cut out to save the mill;
  An', when the wind swung round into the East,
An' blew the roarin' flames along the spur,
Straight for "The Height", I gets quick fear for Her.

Flat out I was with fightin' all day long—
  (We saved the mill-shed, but the huts were done)—
When some bloke, weak with sprintin', comes along—
  (Comic, it seemed to me, the way he run)—
Shoutin' that someone's missin' from "The Height",
An' all the forest at the back's alight.

125

I don't know what he thought, an' never cared,
  When I grabs at his coat, an' starts to yell.
I only know that I was dreadful scared. . . .
  In half a minute more, I guessed 'twas Nell.
He tells me when an' where they thought she went,
An' of the useless searchers they had sent.

I never waits for more; but turned an' ran
  Straight for the spur, along the scorchin' track.
Behind me, as I went, I hear some man—
  I think it's Pike—bawlin', "You fool! Come back!"
What plan was in my mind I cannot tell;
I only know I want to find my Nell.

Next thing I mind, I've left the track, an' turned
  Into the blackened scrub—my eyes feel bad—
Above my head the messmate trees still burned.
  An' Lord, them awful fancies that I had!
I seen her lyin' there—her face—her hair. . . .
Why, even now, them thoughts give me a scare.

I stumble on. Against a red-hot butt
  I burn my hand, but never even swear;
But keep on sayin', "Make the splitter's hut,
  The splitter's hut! Get to the clearin' there.
She's at the splitter's hut; an' if she ain't . . ."
My heart turns over, an' I feel dead faint.

An', as I plug along, I hear some fool
  Repeatin' words till they sound like a spell.
"I'm goin' mad," I thinks. "Keep cool! Keep cool!"
  But still that voice goes on: "My Nell! My Nell!"
I whips round quick to see who he can be,
This yappin' fool—then realize it's me.

I don't know how I reached the splitter's hut,
  I only saw the ragin' fire—an' Nell.
My clothes were torn, my face an' hands were cut,
  An' half a dozen times, at least, I fell.
I burst into the clearin' . . . an' I look. . . .
She's sittin' on a log there—*with a book*!

I seem to cross that clearin' in a stride,
　　Still sobbin' like a kid: "My Nell! My Nell!"
I was clean mad. But, as I reach her side,
　　I sort of wake, an' give that song a spell.
But, by her eyes, for all she seemed so cool,
I know she must have heard, an' feel a fool.

"Why, Mister Jim? You do look hot," says she.
　　(But still her eyes say oceans more than that).
"Did you come all the way up here for me?"
　　Coolness? I tell you straight, it knocked me flat.
By rights, she should fall sobbin' in my arms;
But no; there weren't no shrieks an' no alarms.

I pulls meself together with a jerk.
　　"Oh, just a stroll," I says. "Don't mention it.
The mill's half burnt, an' I am out of work;
　　They missed you, so I looked around a bit."
"Now, that *was* good of you," says she, reel bright.
"Wasn't the bush-fire just a splendid sight?"

She looks me up an' down. "Why, Mister Jim,"
　　She says to me, "you do look hot, indeed.
If you go strollin' that way for a whim
　　Whatever would you do in case of need?"
That's what she said. But with her eyes she sent
More than her thanks; an' I was quite content.

I seen her home; or, rather, she seen me,
　　For I was weak, an' fumbled in my stride.
But, when we reached "The Height", I seen that she
　　Was just on breakin'; an' she went inside. . . .
I stumbles home. "Well, Jim, lad, anyway,"
I tells myself, "you've had a fine, full day."

GREY THRUSH

GREY thrush was in the wattle tree, an', "Oh, you pretty dear!"
He says in his allurin' way; an' I remarks, "Hear, hear!
    That does me nicely for a start; but what do I say next?"
    But then the Jacks take up the song, an' I get very vexed.

The thrush was in the wattle tree, an' I was underneath.
I'd put a clean white collar on, I'd picked a bunch of heath;
    For I was cleaned an' clobbered up to meet my Nell that day.
    But now my awful trouble comes: What is a man to say?

I mean to tell her all I've thought since first I saw her there,
On the bark-heap by the mill-shed, with the sunlight in her hair.
    I mean to tell her all I've done an' what I'll do with life;
    An', when I've said all that an' more, I'll ask her for my wife.

I mean to tell her she's too good, by far, for such as me,
An' how with lonely forest life she never may agree.
    I mean to tell her lots of things, an' be reel straight an' fine;
    And, after she's considered that, I'll ask her to be mine.

I don't suppose I've got much hope—a simple country yob.
I'd like to have a word with Blair—He's wise, is good old Bob;
    He's got such common sense an' that, he'd tip me what to say.
    But I'm not nervous, not a bit; I'll do it my own way. . . .

I seen her by the sassafras, the sun was on her hair;
An' I don't know what come to me to see her standin' there.
    I never even lifts my hat, I never says "Good day"
    To her that should be treated in a reel respectful way.

I only know the girl I want is standin' smilin' there
Right underneath the sassafras. I never thought I'd dare,
    But I holds out my arms to her, an' says, as I come near—
    Not one word of that speech of mine—but, "Oh, you pretty dear!"

It was enough. Lord save a man! It's simple if he knew
There's one way with a woman if she loves you good an' true.
   Next moment she is in my arms; an' me? I don't know where.
   If Heaven can compare with it I won't fret much up there.

"Why, Mister Jim," she says to me. "You're very bold," says she.
"Yes, miss," I says. Then she looks up—an' that's the end of me . . .
   "O man!" she cries. "O modest man, if you go on like this—"
   But I interrupt a lady, an' I do it with a kiss.

"Jim, do you know what heroes are?" says she, when I'd "behaved".
"Why, yes," says I. "They're blokes that save fair maids that won't
      be saved."
   "You're mine," says she, an' smiles at me, "an' will be all my life—
   That is, if it occurs to you to ask me for your wife."

                    .   .   .   .

Grey thrush is in the wattle tree when I get home that day—
Back to my silent, lonely house—an' still he sings away.
   There is no other voice about, no step upon the floor;
   An' none to come an' welcome me as I get to the door.

Yet in the happy heart of me I play at make-believe:
I hear one singin' in the room where once I used to grieve;
   I hear a light step on the path, an', as I reach the gate,
   A happy voice, that makes me glad, tells me I'm awful late.

Now what's a man to think of that, an' what's a man to say,
Who's been out workin' in the bush, tree-fallin', all the day?
   An' how's a man to greet his wife, if she should meet him here?
   But Grey Thrush in the wattle tree says, "Oh, you pretty dear!"

THE GLUGS OF GOSH

[This remarkable mingling of fantasy and satire, published in 1918, appears to have had its origin in some verses which Dennis wrote for a boy, the younger son of J. G. Roberts, to cheer him while in hospital. It developed into a pungent and witty commentary on society in general and the governmental service in particular. (Later again the poet scarified Jacks-in-office in a set of verses entitled "The Jaks of Oss".) There is much smooth and clever writing in The Glugs, notably in the story of Emily Ann. The book contains, moreover, further manifestation of the author's awareness of national danger—a feeling shared by Henry Lawson and certain other writers of the period. Because of the connected nature of the Glug story, the greater part of the little book is given in the extracts that follow.]

· HAL GYE ·

THE GLUG QUEST

FOLLOW the river and cross the ford,
  Follow again to the wobbly bridge,
Turn to the left at the notice-board,
  Climbing the cow-track over the ridge;
Tip-toe soft by the little red house,
  Hold your breath if they touch the latch,
Creep to the slip-rails, still as a mouse,
  Then . . . run like mad for the bracken patch.

Worm your way where the fern-fronds tall
  Fashion a lace-work over your head,
Hemming you in with a high, green wall;
  Then, when the thrush calls once, stop dead.
Ask of the old grey wallaby there—
  Him prick-eared by a woollybutt tree—
How to encounter a Glug, and where
  The country of Gosh, famed Gosh, may be.

  But if he is scornful, if he is dumb,
  Hush! There's another way left. Then come.

On a white, still night, where the dead tree bends
  Over the track, like a waiting ghost
Travel the winding road that wends
  Down to the shore on an Eastern coast.
Follow it down where the wake of the moon
  Kisses the ripples of silver sand;
Follow it on where the night seas croon
  A traveller's tale to the listening land.

Step not jauntily, not too grave,
  Till the lip of the languorous sea you greet;
Wait till the wash of the thirteenth wave
  Tumbles a jellyfish out at your feet.
Not too hopefully, not forlorn,
  Whisper a word of your earnest quest;
Shed not a tear if he turns in scorn
  And sneers in your face like a fish possessed.

133

Hist! Hope on! There is yet a way.
Brooding jellyfish won't be gay.

Wait till the clock in the tower booms three,
   And the big bank opposite gnashes its doors,
Then glide with a gait that is carefully free
   By the great brick building of seventeen floors;
Haste by the draper who smirks at his door,
   Straining to lure you with sinister force,
Turn up the lane by the second-hand store,
   And halt by the light bay carrier's horse.

By the carrier's horse with the long, sad face
   And the wisdom of years in his mournful eye;
Bow to him thrice with a courtier's grace,
   Proffer your query, and pause for reply.
Eagerly ask for a hint of the Glug,
   Pause for reply with your hat in your hand;
If he responds with a snort and a shrug
   Strive to interpret and understand.

   Rare will a carrier's horse condescend.
   Yet there's another way. On to the end!

Catch the four-thirty; your ticket in hand,
   Punched by the porter who broods in his box;
Journey afar to the sad, soggy land,
   Wearing your shot-silk lavender socks;
Wait at the creek by the moss-grown log
   Till the blood of a slain day reddens the West.
Hark for the croak of a gentleman frog,
   Of a corpulent frog with a white satin vest.

Go as he guides you, over the marsh,
   Treading with care on the slithery stones,
Heedless of night winds moaning and harsh
   That seize you and freeze you and search for your bones.
On to the edge of a still, dark pool,
   Banishing thoughts of your warm wool rug;
Gaze in the depths of it, placid and cool,
   And long in your heart for one glimpse of a Glug.

"Krock!" Was he mocking you? "Krock! Kor-r-rock!"
Well, you bought a return, and it's past ten o'clock.

Choose you a night when the intimate stars
  Carelessly prattle of cosmic affairs.
Flat on your back, with your nose pointing Mars,
  Search for the star who fled South from the Bears.
Gaze for an hour at that little blue star,
  Giving him, cheerfully, wink for his wink;
Shrink to the size of the being you are;
  Sneeze if you have to, but softly; then think.

Throw wide the portals and let your thoughts run
  Over the earth like a galloping herd.
Bounds to profundity let there be none,
  Let there be nothing too madly absurd.
Ponder on pebbles or stock exchange shares,
  On the mission of man or the life of a bug,
On planets or billiards, policemen or bears,
  Alert all the time for the sight of a Glug.

Meditate deeply on softgoods or sex,
  On carraway seeds or the causes of bills,
Biology, art, or mysterious wrecks,
  Or the tattered white fleeces of clouds on blue hills.
Muse upon ologies, freckles and fog,
  Why hermits live lonely and grapes in a bunch,
On the ways of a child or the mind of a dog,
  Or the oyster you bolted last Friday at lunch.

  Heard you no sound like a shuddering sigh?
  Or the great shout of laughter that swept down the sky?
  Saw you no sign on the wide Milky Way?
  Then there's naught left to you now but to pray.

Sit you at eve when the Shepherd in Blue
  Calls from the West to his clustering sheep,
Then pray for the moods that old mariners woo,
  For the thoughts of young mothers who watch their babes
    sleep.

Pray for the heart of an innocent child,
  For the tolerant scorn of a weary old man,
For the petulant grief of a prophet reviled,
  For the wisdom you lost when your whiskers began.

Pray for the pleasures that he who was you
  Found in the mud of a shower-fed pool,
For the fears that he felt and the joys that he knew
  When a little green lizard crept into the school.
Pray as they pray who are maddened by wine:
  For distraction from self and a spirit at rest.
Now, deep in the heart of you search for a sign—
  If there be naught of it, vain is your quest.

  Lay down the book, for to follow the tale
  Were to trade in false blame, as all mortals who fail.
  And may the gods salve you on life's dreary round;
  For 'tis whispered: "Who finds not, 'tis he shall be found!"

JOI, THE GLUG

THE Glugs abide in a far, far land
That is partly pebbles and stones and sand,
  But mainly earth of a chocolate hue,
  When it isn't purple or slightly blue.
And the Glugs live there with their aunts and wives,
In draught-proof tenements all their lives.
  And they climb the trees when the weather is wet,
  To see how high they can really get.
        Pray, don't forget,
  This is chiefly done when the weather is wet.

  And every shadow that flits and hides,
  And every stream that glistens and glides
    And laughs its way from a highland height,
    All know the Glugs quite well by sight.
  And they say, "Our test is the best by far;
  For a Glug is a Glug; so there you are!
    And they climb the trees when it drizzles or hails
    To get electricity into their nails;
        And the Glug that fails
    Is a luckless Glug, if it drizzles or hails."

Now, the Glugs abide in the land of Gosh;
And they work all day for the sake of Splosh.
  For Splosh, the First, is the nation's pride,
  And King of the Glugs on his uncle's side.
And they sleep at night, for the sake of rest,
For their doctors say this suits them best.
  And they climb the trees, as a general rule,
  For exercise, when the weather is cool.
        They're taught at school
  To climb the trees when the weather is cool.

  And the whispering grass on the gay green hills,
  And every cricket that skirls and shrills,
    And every moonbeam, gleaming white,
    All know the Glugs quite well by sight.
  And they say, "It is safe, is the test we bring;

For a Glug is an awfully Gluglike thing.
  And they climb the trees when there's sign of a fog,
  To scan the land for a feasible dog;
    They love to jog
  Thro' dells in quest of a feasible dog."

The Glugs eat meals three times a day
Because their fathers ate that way;
  Their grandpas said the scheme was good
  To help the Glugs digest their food.
And 'tis wholesome food the Glugs have got
For it says so plain on the tin and pot.
  And they climb the trees when the weather is dry
  To get a glimpse of the pale green sky.
      We don't know why,
  But they like to gaze on a pale green sky.

And every cloud that sails aloft,
And every breeze that blows so soft,
  And every star that shines at night,
  All know the Glugs quite well by sight.
For they say, "Our test, it is safe and true;
What one Glug does, the other Glugs do;
  And they climb the trees when the weather is hot
  For a bird's-eye view of the garden plot.
      Of course, it's rot,
  But they love that view of the garden plot."

At half-past two on a Wednesday morn
A most peculiar Glug was born;
  And, later on, when he grew a man,
  He scoffed and sneered at the Chosen Plan.
"It's wrong!" said this Glug, whose name was Joi.
"Bah!" said the Glugs. "He's a crazy boy!"
  And they climbed the trees, as the West wind stirred,
  To hark to the note of the Guffer Bird.
      It seems absurd,
  But they're foolishly fond of the Guffer Bird.

And every reed that rustles and sways
By the gurgling river that plashes and plays,
  And the beasts of the dread, neurotic night
  All know the Glugs quite well by sight.
And, "Why," say they; "It is easily done;
For a dexter Glug's like a sinister one!"
  And they climb the trees. Oh, they climb the trees!
  And they bark their knuckles and chafe their knees;
  And 'tis one of the world's great mysteries
          That things like these
Get into, serious histories.

THE STONES OF GOSH

Now, here is a tale of the Glugs of Gosh,
And a wonderful tale I ween,
　　Of the Glugs of Gosh and their great King Splosh
　　And Tush, his virtuous Queen.
And here is a tale of the crafty Ogs,
　　In the neighbouring land of Podge;
Of their sayings and doings and plottings and brewings,
　　And something about Sir Stodge.
　　　　Wise to profundity,
　　　　Stout to rotundity,
　　That was the Knight, Sir Stodge.

Oh, the King was rich, and the Queen was fair,
And they made a very respectable pair.
　　And whenever a Glug in that peaceful land,
　　Did anything no one could understand,
The Knight, Sir Stodge, he looked in a book,
And charged that Glug with the crime called Crook;
　　And the great Judge Fudge, who wore for a hat
　　The sacred skin of a tortoiseshell cat,
He fined that Glug for his action rash,
And frequently asked a deposit in cash.
　　Then every Glug, he went home to his rest
　　With his head in a bag and his toes to the West;
　　　　For they knew it was best,
　　Since their grandpas slept with their toes to the West.

But all of the tale that is so far told
　　Has nothing whatever to do
With the Ogs of Podge, and their crafty dodge,
　　And the trade in pickles and glue.
To trade with the Glugs came the Ogs to Gosh,
　　And they said in seductive tones,

"We'll sell you pianers and pickles and spanners
  For seventeen shiploads of stones:
      Smooth 'uns or nobbly 'uns,
      Firm 'uns or wobbly 'uns,
  All that we ask is stones."

And the King said, "What?" and the Queen said, "Why,
That is awfully cheap to the things I buy!
  For that grocer of ours in the light brown hat
  Asks two and eleven for pickles like that!"
But a Glug stood up with a wart on his nose,
And cried, "Your Majesties! Ogs is foes!"
  But the Glugs cried, "Peace! Will you hold your jaw!
  How did our grandpas fashion the law?"

Said the Knight, Sir Stodge, as he opened his Book,
"When the goods were cheap then the goods they took."
  So they fined the Glug with the wart on his nose
  For wearing a wart with his everyday clothes.
And the goods were bought thro' a Glug named Ghones,
And the Ogs went home with their loads of stones,
      Which they landed with glee in the land of Podge.
      Do you notice the dodge?
  Nor yet did the Glugs, nor the Knight, Sir Stodge.

In the following Summer the Ogs came back
  With a cargo of eight-day clocks,
And hand-painted screens, and sewing machines,
  And mangles, and scissors, and socks.
And they said, "For these excellent things we bring
  We are ready to take more stones;
      And in bricks or road-metal
      For goods you will settle
  Indented by your Mister Ghones."
      Cried the Glugs praisingly,
      "Why, how amazingly
  Smart of industrious Ghones!"

And the King said, "Hum," and the Queen said, "Oo!
That curtain! What a bee—ootiful blue!"
    But a Glug stood up with some very large ears,
    And said, "There is more in this thing than appears!
And we ought to be taxing these goods of the Ogs,
Or our industries soon will be gone to the dogs."
    And the King said, "Bosh! You're un-Gluggish and rude!"
    And the Queen said, "What an absurd attitude!"
Then the Glugs cried, "Down with political quacks!
How did our grandpas look at a tax?"
    So the Knight, Sir Stodge, he opened his Book,
    "No tax," said he, "wherever I look."
Then they fined the Glug with the prominent ears
For being old-fashioned by several years;
    And the Ogs went home with the stones, full-steam.
            Do you notice the scheme?
    Nor yet did the Glugs in their dreamiest dream.

Then every month to the land of Gosh
    The Ogs, they continued to come,
With buttons and hooks, and medical books,
    And rotary engines, and rum,
Large cases with labels, occasional tables,
    Hair tonic, and fiddles and 'phones;
And the Glugs, while concealing their joy in the dealing,
    Paid promptly in nothing but stones.
            Why, it was screamingly
            Laughable, seemingly—
    Asking for nothing but stones!

And the King said, "Haw!" and the Queen said, "Oh!
Our drawing-room now is a heavenly show
    Of large overmantels, and whatnots, and chairs,
    And a statue of Splosh at the head of the stairs!"
But a Glug stood up with a cast in his eye,
And he said, "Far too many such baubles we buy;
    With all the Gosh factories closing their doors,
    And importers' warehouses lining our shores."
    But the Glugs cried, "Down with such meddlesome fools!

What did our grandpas state in their rules?"
  And the Knight, Sir Stodge, he opened his Book:
  "To Cheapness," he said, "was the road they took."
Then every Glug who was not too fat
Turned seventeen handsprings, and jumped on his hat.
  They fined the Glug with the cast in his eye
  For looking both ways—which he did not deny—
And for having no visible precedent, which
Is a crime in the poor and a fault in the rich.

So the Glugs continued, with greed and glee,
To buy cheap clothing, and pills, and tea;
  Till every Glug in the land of Gosh
  Owned three clean shirts and a fourth in the wash.
But they all grew idle, and fond of ease,
And easy to swindle, and hard to please;
  And the voice of Joi was a lonely voice,
  When he railed at Gosh for its foolish choice.
But the great King grinned, and the good Queen gushed,
As the goods of the Ogs were madly rushed.
  And the Knight, Sir Stodge, with a wave of his hand,
  Declared it a happy and prosperous land.

SYM, THE SON OF JOI

Now, Joi, the rebel, he had a son
  In far, far Gosh where the tall trees wave.
Said Joi: "In Gosh there shall yet be one
  To scorn this life of a self-made slave;
To spurn the law of the Knight, Sir Stodge,
  And end the rule of the great King Splosh;
Who shall warn the Glugs of their crafty dodge,
  And at last bring peace, sweet peace, to Gosh."

Said he: "Whenever the kind sun showers
His golden treasure on grateful flowers,
  With upturned faces and hearts bowed low
  The Glugs shall know what the wild things know."
Said he: "Wherever the broad fields smile
They shall walk with clean minds, free of guile;
  They shall scoff aloud at the call of Greed,
  And turn to their labours and never heed."

So Joi had a son, and his name was Sym,
  And his eyes were wide as the eyes of Truth;
And there came to the wondering mind of him
  Long thoughts of the riddle that vexes youth.
And, "Father," he said, "in the mart's loud din
  Is there aught of pleasure? Do some find joy?"
But his father tilted the beardless chin,
  And looked in the eyes of the questing boy.

Said he: "Whenever the fields are green,
Lie still, where the wild rose fashions a screen,
  While the brown thrush calls to his love-wise mate,
  And know what they profit who trade with Hate."
Said he: "Whenever the great skies spread,
In the beckoning vastness overhead,
  A tent for the blue wren building a nest,
  Then, down in the heart of you, learn what's best."

144

And there came to Sym as he walked afield
  Deep thoughts of the world and the folk of Gosh.
He saw the idols to which they kneeled;
  He marked them cringe to the name of Splosh.
"Is it meet," he asked, "that a soul should crawl
  To a purple robe or a gilded chair?"
But his father walked to the garden's wall
  And stooped to a rose-bush flowering there.

Said he: "Whenever a bursting bloom
Looks up to the sun, may a soul find room
  For a measure of awe at the wondrous birth
  Of one more treasure to this glad earth."
Said he: "Whenever a dewdrop clings
To a gossamer thread, and glitters and swings,
  Deep in humility bow your head
  To a thing for a blundering mortal's dread."

And there came to Sym in his later youth,
  With the first clear glance in the face of guile,
Thirst for knowledge and thoughts of truth,
  Of gilded baubles, and things worth while.
And he said, "There is much that a Glug should know;
  But his mind is clouded, his years are few."
Then, Joi, the father, he answered low,
  As his thoughts ran back to the youth he knew.

Said he: "Whenever the West wind stirs,
And birds in feathers and beasts in furs
  Steal out to dance in the glade, lie still:
  Let your heart teach you what it will."
Said he: "Whenever the moonlight creeps
Thro' inlaced boughs, and a shy star peeps
  Adown from its crib in the cradling sky,
  Know of their folly who fear to die."

145

New interest came to the mind of Sym,
　　As 'midst his fellows he lived and toiled.
But the ways of the Glug folk puzzled him;
　　For some won honour, while some were foiled;
Yet all were filled with a vague unrest
　　As they climbed their trees in an endless search.
But Joi, the father, he mocked their quest,
　　When he marked a Glug on his hard-won perch.

As he walked in the city, to Sym there came
　　Sounds envenomed with fear and hate,
Shouts of anger and words of shame,
　　As Glug blamed Glug for his woeful state.
"This blame?" said Sym, "Is it mortal's right
　　To blame his fellow for aught he be?"
But the father said, "Do we blame the night
　　When the darkness gathers and none can see?"

　　　　・　　・　　・　　・　　・　　・　　・

So Joi had a son, and his name was Sym;
　　Far from the ken of the great King Splosh.
And small was the Glug's regard of him,
　　Mooning along in the streets of Gosh;
But many a creature by field and ford
　　Shared in the schooling of that strange boy,
Dreaming and planning to gather and hoard
　　Knowledge of all things precious to Joi.

THE GROWTH OF SYM

Now, Sym was a Glug; and 'tis mentioned so
That the tale reads perfectly plain as we go.
  In his veins ran blood of that stupid race
  Of docile folk, who inhabit the place
Called Gosh, sad Gosh, where the tall trees sigh
With a strange, significant sort of cry
When the gloaming creeps and the wind is high.

When the deep shades creep and the wind is high
The trees bow low as the gods ride by:
  Gods of the gloaming, who ride on the breeze,
  Stooping to hearten the birds and the trees.
But each dull Glug sits down by his door,
And mutters, " 'Tis windy!" and nothing more,
Like the long-dead Glugs in the days of yore.

When Sym was born there was much to-do,
And his parents thought him a joy to view;
  But folk not prejudiced saw the Glug,
  As his nurse remarked, "In the cut of his mug."
For he had their hair, and he had their eyes,
And the Glug expression of pained surprise,
And their predilection for pumpkin pies.

And his parents' claims were a deal denied
By his maiden aunt on his mother's side,
  A tall Glug lady of fifty-two
  With a slight moustache of an auburn hue.
"Parental blither!" she said quite flat.
"He's an average Glug; and he's red and fat!
And exceedingly fat and red at that!"

But the father, Joi, when he gazed on Sym,
Dreamed great and wonderful things for him.
   Said he, "If the mind of a Glug could wake
   Then, Oh, what a wonderful Glug he'd make!
We shall teach this laddie to play life's game
With a different mind and a definite aim:
A Glug in appearance, yet not the same."

But the practical aunt said, "Fudge! You fool!
We'll pack up his dinner and send him to school.
   He shall learn about two-times and parsing and capes,
   And how to make money with inches on tapes.
We'll apprentice him then to the drapery trade,
Where, I've heard it reported, large profits are made;
Besides, he can sell us cheap buttons and braid."

So poor young Sym, he was sent to school,
   "Do unto others," the teacher said . . .
   Then suddenly stopped and scratched his head.
"You may look up the rest in a book," said he.
"At present it doesn't occur to me;
But do it, whatever it happens to be."

"And now," said the teacher, "the day's task brings
Consideration of practical things.
   If a man makes a profit of fifteen pounds
   On one week's takings from two milk rounds,
How many . . . ?" And Sym went dreaming away
To the sunlit lands where the field-mice play,
And wrens hold revel the livelong day.

He walked in the welcoming fields alone,
While from far, far away came the pedagogue's drone:
   "If a man makes . . . Multiply . . . Abstract nouns . . .
   From B take . . . Population of towns . . .
Rods, poles or perches . . . Derived from Greek . . ."
Oh, the hawthorn buds came out this week,
And robins are nesting down by the creel.

So Sym was head of his class not once;
And his aunt repeatedly dubbed him "Dunce!"
    But, "Give him a chance," said his father, Joi,
    "His head is abnormally large for a boy."
But his aunt said, "Piffle! It's crammed with bosh!
Why, he don't know the rivers and mountains of Gosh,
Nor the names of the nephews of good King Splosh!"

In Gosh, when a youth gets an obstinate look,
And copies his washing-bill into a book,
    And blackens his boot-heels, and frowns at a joke,
    "Ah, he's getting sense," say the elderly folk.
But Sym, he would laugh when he ought to be sad;
Said his aunt, "Lawk-a-mussy! What's wrong with the lad?
He romps with the puppies, and talks to the ants,
    And keeps his loose change in his second-best pants,
    And stumbles all over my cauliflow'r plants!"

"There is wisdom in that," laughed the father, Joi.
But the aunt said, "Toity!" and, "Drat the boy!"
    "He shall play," said the father, "some noble part.
    Who knows but it may be in letters or art?
'Tis a dignified business to make folk think."
But the aunt cried, "What! Go messing with ink,
And smear all his fingers, and take to drink,
Paint hussies and cows, and end in the clink?"

So the argument ran; but one bright Spring day
Sym settled it all in his own strange way.
    "'Tis a tramp," he announced, "I've decided to be;
    And I start next Monday at twenty to three . . ."
When the aunt recovered she screamed, "A tramp?
A low-lived, pilfering, idle scamp,
Who steals people's washing, and sleeps in the damp?"

Sharp to the hour Sym was ready and dressed.
"Young birds," sighed the father, "must go from the nest.
    When the green moss covers those stones you tread,
    When the green grass whispers above my head,
Mark well, wherever your path may turn,
They have reached the valley of peace who learn
That wise hearts cherish what fools may spurn."

So Sym went off; and a year ran by,
And the father said, with a smile-masked sigh,
   "It is meet that the young should leave the nest."
   Said the aunt, "Don't spill that soup on your vest!
Nor mention his name! He's our one disgrace!
And he's probably sneaking around some place
With fuzzy black whiskers all over his face."

But, under a hedge, by a flowering peach,
A youth with a little blue wren held speech.
   With his back to a tree and his feet in the grass,
   He watched the thistle-down drift and pass,
And the cloud-puffs, borne on a lazy breeze,
Move by on their errand, above the trees,
Into the vault of the mysteries.

"Now, teach me, little blue wren," said he.
" Tis you can unravel this riddle for me.
   I am 'mazed by the gifts of this kindly earth—
   Which of them all has the greatest worth?"
He flirted his tail as he answered then,
He bobbed and he bowed to his coy little hen:
"Why, sunlight and worms!" said the little blue wren.

THE SWANKS OF GOSH

COME mourn with me for the land of Gosh,
  Oh, weep with me for the luckless Glugs
Of the land of Gosh, where the sad seas wash
The patient shores, and the great King Splosh
     His sodden sorrow hugs;
Where the fair Queen Tush weeps all the day,
  And the Swank, the Swank, the naughty Swank,
     The haughty Swank holds sway—
The most·mendacious, ostentatious,
     Spacious Swank holds sway.

Tis sorrow-swathed, as I know full well,
  And garbed in gloom and the weeds of woe,
And vague, so far, is the tale I tell;
But bear with me for the briefest spell,
     And surely shall ye know
Of the land of Gosh, and Tush, and Splosh,
  And Stodge, the Swank, the foolish Swank,
     The mulish Swank of Gosh—
The meretricious, avaricious,
     Vicious Swank of Gosh.

Oh, the tall trees bend, and green trees send
  A chuckle round the earth,
And the soft winds croon a jeering tune,
  And the harsh winds shriek with mirth;
And the wee small birds chirp ribald words
  When the Swank walks down the street;
But every Glug takes off his hat,
And whispers humbly, "Look at that!
  Hats off! Hats off to the Glug of rank!
  Sir Stodge, the Swank, the Lord High Swank!"
Then the East wind roars a loud guffaw,
And the haughty Swank says, "Haw!"

In Gosh, sad Gosh, where the Lord Swank lives,
   He holds high rank, and he has much pelf;
And all the well-paid posts he gives
Unto his fawning relatives,
      As foolish as himself.
In offices and courts and boards
   Are Swanks, and Swanks, ten dozen Swanks,
      And cousin Swanks in hordes—
Inept and musty, dry and dusty,
      Rusty Swanks in hordes.

They lurk in every Gov'ment lair,
   'Mid docket dull and dusty file,
Solemnly squat in an easy chair,
Penning a minute of rare hot air
      In departmental style.
In every office, on every floor
   Are Swanks, and Swanks, distracting Swanks,
      And Acting-Swanks a score,
And coldly distant, sub-assistant
      Under-Swanks galore.

The tall trees sway like boys at play,
   And mock him when he grieves,
As one by one, in laughing fun,
   They pelt him with their leaves.
And the gay green trees joke to the breeze,
   As the Swank struts proudly by;
But every Glug, with reverence,
Pays homage to his pride immense—
   A homage deep to lofty rank—
   The Swank! The Swank! The pompous Swank!
But the wind-borne leaves await their chance
      And round him gaily dance.

Now, trouble came to the land of Gosh:
   The fear of battle, and anxious days;
And the Swanks were called to the great King Splosh,
Who said that their system would not wash,
      And ordered other ways.
Then the Lord High Swank stretched forth a paw,

And penned a minute *re* the law,
  And the Swanks, the Swanks, the other Swanks,
    The brother Swanks said, "Haw!"
These keen, resourceful, unremorseful,
    Forceful Swanks said, "Haw!"

Then Splosh, the king, in a royal rage,
  He smote his throne as he thundered, "Bosh!
In the whole wide land is there not one sage
With a cool, clear brain, who'll straight engage
    To sweep the Swanks from Gosh?"
But the Lord High Stodge, from where he stood,
Cried, "Barley! . . . Guard your livelihood!"
  And, quick as light, the teeming Swanks,
    The scheming Swanks touched wood.
Sages, plainly, labour vainly
    When the Swanks touch wood.

The stealthy cats that grace the mats
  Before the doors of Gosh,
Smile wide with scorn each sunny morn;
  And, as they take their wash,
A sly grimace o'erspreads each face
  As the Swank struts forth to court.
But every Glug casts down his eyes,
And mutters, "Ain't 'is 'at a size!
  For such a sight our gods we thank.
  Sir Stodge, the Swank! The noble Swank!"
But the West wind tweaks his nose in sport;
  And the Swank struts into court.

Then roared the King with a rage intense,
  "Oh, who can cope with their magic tricks?"
But the Lord High Swank skipped nimbly hence,
And hid him safe behind the fence
    Of Regulation VI.
And under Section Four Eight O
The Swanks, the Swanks, dim forms of Swanks,
    The swarms of Swanks lay low—
These most tenacious, perspicacious,
    Spacious Swanks lay low.

Cried the King of Gosh, "They shall not escape!
  Am I set at naught by a crazed buffoon?"
But in fifty fathoms of thin red tape
The Lord Swank swaddled his portly shape,
    Like a large, insane cocoon.
Then round and round and round and round
  The Swanks, the Swanks, the whirling Swanks,
    The twirling Swanks they wound—
The swathed and swaddled, molly-coddled
    Swanks inanely wound.

Each insect thing that comes in Spring
  To gladden this sad earth,
It flits and whirls and pipes and skirls,
  It chirps in mocking mirth
A merry song the whole day long
  To see the Swank abroad.
But every Glug, whoe'er he be,
Salutes, with grave humility
  And deference to noble rank,
  The Swank, the Swank, the swollen Swank;
But the South wind blows his clothes awry,
    And flings dust in his eye.

So trouble stayed in the land of Gosh;
  And the futile Glugs could only gape,
While the Lord High Swank still ruled King Splosh
With laws of blither and rules of bosh,
    From out his lair of tape.
And in cocoons that mocked the Glug
  The Swanks, the Swanks, the under-Swanks,
    The dunder Swanks lay snug.
These most politic, parasitic,
    Critic Swanks lay snug.

Then mourn with me for a luckless land,
  Oh, weep with me for the slaves of tape!
Where the Lord High Swank still held command,
And wrote new rules in a fair round hand,
    And the Glugs saw no escape;

Where tape entwined all Gluggish things,
        And the Swank, the Swank, the grievous Swank,
            The devious Swank pulled strings—
    The perspicacious, contumacious
            Swank held all the strings.

The blooms that grow, and, in a row,
  Peep o'er each garden fence,
They nod and smile to note his style
  Of ponderous pretence;
Each roving bee has fits of glee
  When the Swank goes by that way.
But every Glug, he makes his bow,
And says, "Just watch him! Watch him now!
  He must have thousands in the bank!
  The Swank! The Swank! The holy Swank!"
But the wild winds snatch his kerchief out,
        And buffet him about.

THE SEER

SOMEWHERE or other, 'tis doubtful where,
In the archives of Gosh is a volume rare,
  A precious old classic that nobody reads,
  And nobody asks for, and nobody heeds;
Which makes it a classic, and famed thro' the land,
As well-informed persons will quite understand.

'Tis a ponderous work, and 'tis written in prose.
For some mystical reason that nobody knows;
  And it tells in a style that is terse and correct
  Of the rule of the Swanks and its baneful effect
On the commerce of Gosh, on its morals and trade;
And it quotes a grave prophecy somebody made.

And this is the prophecy, written right bold
On a parchment all tattered and yellow and old;
  So old and so tattered that nobody knows
  How far into foretime its origin goes.
But this is the writing that set Glugs agog
When 'twas called to their minds by the Mayor of Quog:

When Gosh groaneth vastlie thro Greed and hys plannes
Ye rimer shall mende ye who mendes pottes and pans.

Now, the Mayor of Quog, a small suburb of Gosh,
Was intensely annoyed at the act of King Splosh
  In asking the Mayor of Piphel to tea
  With himself and the Queen on a Thursday at three;
When the King must have known that the sorriest dog,
If a native of Piphel, was hated in Quog.

An act without precedent! Quog was ignored!
The Mayor and Council and Charity Board,
  They met and considered this insult to Quog;
  And they said, " 'Tis the work of the treacherous Og!
'Tis plain the Og influence threatens the Throne;
And the Swanks are all crazed with this trading in stone."

Said the Mayor of Quog: "This has long been foretold
In a prophecy penned by the Seer of old.
    We must search, if we'd banish the curse of our time,
    For a mender of pots who's a maker of rhyme.
'Tis to him we must look when our luck goes amiss.
But, Oh, where in all Gosh is a Glug such as this?"

Then the Mayor and Council and Charity Board
O'er the archival prophecy zealously pored,
    With a pursing of lips and a shaking of heads,
    With a searching and prying for possible threads
That would lead to discover this versatile Glug
Who modelled a rhyme while he mended a mug.

With a pursing of lips and a shaking of heads,
They gave up the task and went home to their beds,
    Where each lay awake while he tortured his brain
    For a key to the riddle, but ever in vain . . .
Then, lo, at the Mayor's front door in the morn
A tinker called out, and a Movement was born.

"Kettles and pans! Kettles and pans!
Oh, the stars are the gods'; but the earth, it is man's.
    But a fool is the man who has wants without end,
    While the tinker's content with a kettle to mend.
For a tinker owns naught but the earth, which is man's.
Then, bring out your kettles! Ho, kettles and pans!"

From the mayoral bed with unmayoral cries
The magistrate sprang ere he'd opened his eyes.
    "Hold him!" he yelled, as he bounced on the floor.
    "Oh, who is this tinker that rhymes at my door?
Go get me the name and the title of him!"
They answered, "Be calm, sir. 'Tis no one but Sym.

" 'Tis Sym, the mad tinker, the son of old Joi,
Who ran from his home when a bit of a boy.
    He went for a tramp, tho' 'tis common belief,
    When folk were not looking he went for a thief;
Then went for a tinker, and rhymes as he goes.
Some say he's crazy, but nobody knows."

'Twas thus it began, the exalting of Sym,
And the mad Gluggish struggle that raged around him.
  For the good Mayor seized him, and clothed him in silk,
  And fed him on pumpkins and pasteurised milk,
And praised him in public, and coupled his name
With Gosh's vague prophet of archival fame.

The Press interviewed him a great many times,
And printed his portrait, and published his rhymes;
  Till the King and Sir Stodge and the Swanks grew afraid
  Of his fame 'mid the Glugs and the trouble it made.
For, wherever Sym went in the city of Gosh,
There were cheers for the tinker, and hoots for King Splosh.

His goings and comings were watched for and cheered;
And a crowd quickly gathered where'er he appeared.
  All the folk flocked around him and shouted his praise;
  For the Glugs followed fashion, and Sym was a craze.
They sued him for words, which they greeted with cheers,
For the way with a Glug is to tickle his ears.

"O, speak to us, Tinker! Your wisdom we crave!"
They'd cry when they saw him; then Sym would look grave,
  And remark, with an air, "'Tis a very fine day."
  "Now ain't he a marvel?" they'd shout. "Hip, Hooray!"
"To live," would Sym answer, "To live is to feel!"
"And ain't he a poet?" a fat Glug would squeal.

Sym had a quaint fancy in phrase and in text;
When he'd fed them with one they would howl for the next.
  Thus he'd cry, "Love is love!" and the welkin they'd lift
  With their shouts of surprise at his wonderful gift.
He would say "After life, then a Glug must meet death!"
And they'd clamour for more ere he took the next breath.

But Sym grew aweary of this sort of praise,
And he longed to be back with his out-o'-door days,
  With his feet in the grass and his back to a tree,
  Rhyming and tinkering, fameless and free.
He said so one day to the Mayor of Quog,
And declared he'd as lief live the life of a dog.

But the Mayor was vexed; for the Movement had grown,
And his dreams had of late soared as high as a throne.
   "Have a care! What is written is written," said he.
   "And the dullest Glug knows what is written must be.
'Tis the prophet of Gosh who has prophesied it;
And 'tis thus that 'tis written by him who so writ:

" 'Lo, the Tinker of Gosh he shall make him three rhymes:
One on the errors and aims of his times,
   One on the symptoms of sin that he sees,
   And the third and the last on whatever he please.
And when the Glugs hear them and mark what they mean
The land shall be purged and the nation made clean.' "

So Sym gave a promise to write then and there
Three rhymes to be read in the Great Market Square
To all Glugs assembled on Saturday week.
"And then," said the Mayor, "if still you must seek
   To return to your tramping, well, just have your fling;
   But I'll make you a marquis, or any old thing . . ."
   Said Sym, "I shall tinker, and still be a king."

THE RHYMES OF SYM

NOBODY knew why it should be so;
Nobody knew or wanted to know.
  It might have been checked had but somebody dared
  To trace its beginnings; but nobody cared.
But 'twas clear to the wise that the Glugs of those days
Were crazed beyond reason concerning a craze.

They would pass a thing by for a week. or a year,
With an air apathetic, or maybe a sneer:
  Some ev'ryday thing, like a crime or a creed,
  A mode or a movement, and pay it small heed,
Till Somebody started to laud it aloud;
Then all but the Nobodies followed the crowd.

Thus, Sym was a craze; tho', to give him his due,
He would rather have strayed from the popular view.
  But once the Glugs had him they held him so tight
  That he could not be nobody, try as he might;
He had to be Somebody, so they decreed,
For Craze is an appetite, governed by Greed.

So on Saturday week to the Great Market Square
Came every Glug who could rake up his fare.
  They came from the suburbs, they came from the town,
  There came from the country Glugs bearded and brown,
Rich Glugs, with cigars, all well-tailored and stout,
Jostled commonplace Glugs who dropped aitches about.

There were gushing Glug maids, well aware of their charms,
And stern, massive matrons with babes in their arms.
  There were querulous dames who complained of the "squash",
  The pushing and squeezing; for, briefly, all Gosh,
With its aunt and its wife, stood agape in the ranks—
Excepting Sir Stodge and his satellite Swanks.

The Mayor of Quog took the chair for the day;
And he made them a speech, and he ventured to say
  That a Glug was a Glug, and the Cause they held dear
  Was a very dear Cause. And the Glugs said, "Hear, hear!"
Then Sym took the stage to a round of applause
From thousands who suddenly found they'd a Cause.

THE FIRST RHYME OF SYM

We strive together in life's crowded mart,
  Keen-eyed, with clutching hands to over-reach;
We scheme, we lie, we play the selfish part,
  Masking our lust for gain with gentle speech;
And masking too—O pity ignorance!—
Our very selves behind a careless glance.

We preach; yet do we deem it worldly-wise
  To count unbounded brother-love a shame,
So, ban the brother-look from out our eyes,
  Lest sparks of sympathy be fanned to flame.
We smile; and yet withhold, in secret fear,
The word so hard to speak, so sweet to hear—

Nay, brothers, look about your world to-day:
  A world to you so drab, so commonplace—
The flowers still are blooming by the way,
  As blossom smiles upon the sternest face.
In every hour is born some thought of love;
In every heart is hid some treasure-trove.

. . . .

With a modified clapping and stamping of feet
The Glugs mildly cheered him, as Sym took his seat.
  But some said 'twas clever, and some said 'twas grand—
  More especially those who did *not* understand.
And some said, with frowns, tho' the words sounded plain,
Yet it had a deep meaning they craved to explain.

But the Mayor said: Silence! He wished to observe
That a Glug was a Glug; and in wishing to serve
  This glorious Cause, which they'd asked him to lead,

161

They had proved they were Glugs of the noble old breed
That made Gosh what it was . . . and he'd ask the police
To remove that small boy while they heard the next piece.

THE SECOND RHYME OF SYM

"Now come," said the Devil, he said to me,
  With his swart face all a-grin,
"This day, ere ever the clock strikes three,
  Shall you sin your darling sin.
For I've wagered a crown with Beelzebub,
Down there at the Gentlemen's Brimstone Club,
  I shall tempt you once, I shall tempt you twice,
  Yet thrice shall you fall ere I tempt you thrice."

"Begone, base Devil!" I made reply—
  Begone with your fiendish grin!
How hope you to profit by such as i?
  For I have no darling sin.
But many there be, and I know them well,
All foul with sinning and ripe for Hell.
  And I name no names, but the whole world knows
  That I am never of such as those."

"How now?" said the Devil. "I'll spread my net,
  And I vow I'll gather you in!
By this and by that shall I win my bet,
  And you shall sin the sin!
Come, fill up a bumper of good red wine,
Your heart shall sing, and your eye shall shine,
  You shall know such joy as you never have known—
  For the salving of men was the good vine grown."

"Begone, red Devil!" I made reply.
  "Parch shall these lips of mine,
And my tongue shall shrink, and my throat go dry,
  Ere ever I taste your wine!
But greet you shall, as I know full well,
A tipsy score of my friends in Hell.
  And I name no names, but the whole world wots
  Most of my fellows are drunken sots."

162

"Ah, ha!" said the Devil. "You scorn the wine!
  Thrice shall you sin, I say,
To win me a crown from a friend of mine,
  Ere three o' the clock this day.
Are you calling to mind some lady fair?
And is she a wife or a maiden rare?
  'Twere folly to shackle young love, hot Youth;
  And stolen kisses are sweet, forsooth!"

"Begone, foul Devil!" I made reply;
  "For never in all my life
Have I looked on a woman with lustful eye,
  Be she maid, or widow, or wife.
But my brothers! Alas! I am scandalized
By their evil passions so ill disguised.
  And I name no names, but my thanks I give
  That I loathe the lives my fellow-men live."

"Ho, ho!" roared the Devil in fiendish glee,
  " 'Tis a silver crown I win!
Thrice have you fallen! O Pharisee,
  You have sinned your darling sin!"
"But, nay," said I; "and I scorn your lure.
I have sinned no sin, and my heart is pure.
  Come, show me a sign of the sin you see!"
  But the Devil was gone . . . and the clock struck three.

· · · · · · ·

With an increase of cheering and waving of hats—
While the little boys squealed, and made noises like cats—
  The Glugs gave approval to Sym's second rhyme.
  And some said 'twas thoughtful, and some said 'twas prime;
And some said 'twas witty, and had a fine end:
More especially those who did *not* comprehend.

And some said with leers and with nudges and shrugs
That, they mentioned no names, but it hit certain Glugs.
  And others remarked, with superior smiles,
  While dividing the metrical feet into miles,
That the thing seemed quite simple, without any doubt,
But the anagrams in it would need thinking out.

But the Mayor said, Hush! And he wished to explain
That in leading this Movement he'd nothing to gain.
  He was ready to lead, since they trusted him so;
  And, wherever he led he was sure Glugs would go.
And he thanked them again, and craved peace for a time,
While this gifted young man read his third and last rhyme.

THE LAST RHYME OF SYM

*(To sing you a song and a sensible song is a worthy and excellent
    thing;*
*But how could I sing you that sort of a song, if there's never a
    song to sing?)*
At ten to the tick, by the kitchen clock, I marked him blundering by,
*With his eyes astare, and his rumpled hair, and his hat cocked
    over his eye.*
Blind, in his pride, to his shoes untied, he went with a swift jig-jog,
Off on the quest, with a strange unrest, hunting the Feasible Dog.
*And this is the song, as he dashed along, that he sang with a
    swaggering swing—*
*(Now how had I heard him singing a song if he hadn't a song to
    sing?)*

> *"I've found the authentic, identical beast!*
> *The Feasible Dog, and the terror of Gosh!*
> *I know by the prowl of him.*
> *Hark to the growl of him!*
> *Heralding death to the subjects of Splosh.*
> *Oh, look at him glaring and staring, by thunder!*
> *Now each for himself, and the weakest goes under!*

> *"Beware this injurious, furious brute;*
> *He's ready to rend you with tooth and with claw.*
> *Tho' 'tis incredible,*
> *Anything edible*
> *Disappears suddenly into his maw:*
> *Into his cavernous inner interior*
> *Vanishes ev'rything strictly superior."*

164

He calls it "Woman", he calls it "Wine", he calls it "Devils" and
    "Dice";
He calls it "Surfing" and "Sunday Golf" and names that are not
    so nice.
But whatever he calls it—"Morals" or "Mirth"—he is on with the
    hunt right quick
For his sorrow he'd hug like a gloomy Glug if he hadn't a dog to
    kick.

. . . .

Such a shouting and yelling of hearty Bravoes,
Such a craning of necks and a standing on toes
    Seemed to leave ne'er a doubt that the Tinker's last rhyme
    Had now won him repute 'mid the Glugs for all time.
And they all said the rhyme was the grandest they'd heard:
More especially those who had not caught a word.

But the Mayor said: Peace! And he stood, without fear,
As the leader of all to whom Justice was dear.
    For the Tinker had rhymed, as the Prophet foretold,
    And a light was let in on the errors of old.
For in every line, and in every verse
Was the proof that Sir Stodge was a traitor, and worse!

Sir Stodge (said the Mayor), must go from his place;
And the Swanks, one and all, were a standing disgrace!
    For the influence won o'er a weak, foolish king
    Was a menace to Gosh, and a scandalous thing!
"And now," said the Mayor, "I stand here to-day
As your leader and friend." And the Glugs said, "Hooray!"

Then they went to their homes in the suburbs and town;
To their farms went the Glugs who were bearded and brown.
    Portly Glugs with cigars went to dine at their clubs,
    While illiterate Glugs had one more at the pubs.
And each household in Gosh sat and talked half the night
Of the wonderful day, and the imminent fight.

Forgetting the rhymer, forgetting his rhymes,
They talked of Sir Stodge and his numerous crimes.
   There was hardly a Glug in the whole land of Gosh
   Who'd a lenient word to put in for King Splosh.
One and all, to the mangiest, surliest dog,
Were quite eager to bark for his Worship of Quog.

Forgotten, unnoticed, Sym wended his way
To his lodging in Gosh at the close of the day.
   And 'twas there, to his friend and companion of years—
   To his little red dog with the funny prick ears—
That he poured out his woe; seeking nothing to hide;
And the little dog listened, his head on one side.

"O you little red dog, you are weary as I.
It is days, it is months since we saw the blue sky.
   And it seems weary years since we sniffed at the breeze
   As it hums thro' the hedges and sings in the trees.
These we know and we love. But this city holds fears,
O my friend of the road, with the funny prick ears.
   And for what may we hope from his Worship of Quog?"
   "Oh, a bone and a kick," said the little red dog.

OGS

I⊤ chanced one day, in the middle of May,
  There came to the great King Splosh
A policeman, who said, while scratching his head,
  "There isn't a stone in Gosh
To throw at a dog; for the crafty Og,
  Last Saturday week, at one,
Took our last blue-metal, in order to settle
  A bill for a toy pop-gun."
      Said the King, jokingly,
      "Why, how provokingly
Weird; but we have the gun."

And the King said, "Well, we are stony broke."
But the Queen could not see it was much of a joke.
  And she said, "If the metal is all used up,
  Pray what of the costume I want for the Cup?
It all seems so dreadfully simple to me.
The stones? Why, import them from over the sea."
  But a Glug stood up with a mole on his chin,
  And said, with a most diabolical grin,
"Your Majesties, down in the country of Podge,
A spy has discovered a very 'cute dodge.
  And the Ogs are determined to wage a war
  On Gosh, next Friday, at half-past four."
Then the Glugs all cried, in a terrible fright,
"How did our grandfathers manage a fight?"

Then the Knight, Sir Stodge, he opened his Book,
And he read, "Some very large stones they took,
  And flung at the foe, with exceeding force;
  Which as very effective, tho' rude, of course."
And lo, with sorrowful wails and moans,
The Glugs cried, "Where, Oh, where are the stones?"
  And some rushed North, and a few ran West;
  Seeking the substitutes seeming best.

And they gathered the pillows and cushions and rugs
From the homes of the rich and middle-class Glugs.
  And a hasty message they managed to send
  Craving the loan of some bricks from a friend.

On the Friday, exactly at half-past four,
  Came the Ogs with triumphant glee.
And the first of their stones hit poor Mister Ghones,
  The captain of industry.
Then a pebble of Podge took the Knight, Sir Stodge,
  In the curve of his convex vest.
He gurgled "Un-Gluggish!" His heart growing sluggish,
  He solemnly sank to rest.
      'Tis inconceivable,
      Scarcely believable,
  Yet, he was sent to rest.

And the King said, "Ouch!" and the Queen said, "Oo!
My bee-ootiful drawing-room! What shall I do?"
  But the warlike Ogs, they hurled great rocks
  Thro' the works of the wonderful eight-day clocks
They had sold to the Glugs but a month before—
Which was very absurd; but, of course, 'twas war.
  And the Glugs cried, "What would our grandfathers do
  If they hadn't the stones that they one time threw?"
But the Knight, Sir Stodge, and his mystic Book
Oblivious slept in a grave-yard nook.

Then a Glug stood out with a pot in his hand,
As the King was bewailing the fate of his land,
  And he said, "If these Ogs you desire to retard,
  Then hit them quite frequent with *anything* hard."
So the Glugs seized anvils, and editors' chairs,
And smote the Ogs with them unawares;
  And bottles of pickles, and clocks they threw,
  And books of poems, and gherkins, and glue,
Which they'd bought with the stones—as, of course, you know—
From the Ogs but a couple of months ago.
  Which was simply inane, when you reason it o'er;
  And uneconomic, but then, it was war.

When they'd fought for a night and the most of a day,
The Ogs threw the last of their metal away.
    Then they went back to Podge, well content with their fun,
    And, with much satisfaction, declared they had won.
And the King of the Glugs gazed around on his land,
And saw nothing but stones strewn on every hand:
    Great stones in the palace, and stones in the street,
    And stones on the house-tops and under the feet.
And he said, with a desperate look on his face,
"There is nothing so ghastly as stones out of place.
    And, no doubt, this Og scheme was a very smart dodge.
    But whom does it profit—my people, or Podge?

EMILY ANN

Government muddled, departments dazed,
Fear and confusion wherever he gazed;
   Order insulted, authority spurned,
   Dread and distraction wherever he turned—
Oh, the great King Splosh was a sad, sore king,
With never a statesman to straighten the thing.

Glugs all importunate urging their claims,
With selfish intent and ulterior aims,
   Glugs with petitions for this and for that,
   Standing ten deep on the royal door-mat,
Raging when nobody answered their ring—
Oh, the Great King Splosh was a careworn king.

And he looked to the right, and he glanced to the left,
And he glared at the roof like a monarch bereft
   Of his wisdom and wits and his wealth all in one;
   And, at least once a minute, asked, "What's to be done?"
But the Swanks stood around him and answered, with groans,
"Your Majesty, Gosh is half buried in stones!"

"How now?" cried the King. "Is there not in my land
One Glug who can cope with this dreadful demand:
   A rich man, a poor man, a beggar man, thief—
   I reck not his rank so he lessen my grief—
A soldier, a sailor, a—?" Raising his head,
With relief in his eye, "Now, I mind me!" he said:

"I mind me a Tinker, and what once befel,
When I think, on the whole, he was treated not well.
   But he shall be honoured, and he shall be famed
   If he read me this riddle. But how is he named?
Some commonplace title, like—Simon?—No—Sym!
Go, send out my riders, and scour Gosh for him."

They rode for a day to the sea in the South,
Calling the name of him, hand to the mouth.
  They rode for a day to the hills in the East,
  But signs of a tinker saw never the least.
Then they rode to the North thro' a whole day long,
And paused in the even to hark to a song.

"Kettles and pans! Kettles and pans!
Oh, who can show tresses like Emily Ann's?
  Brown in the shadow and gold at the tips.
  Bright as the smile on her beckoning lips.
Bring out your kettle! O kettle or pan!
So I buy me a ribband for Emily Ann."

With his feet in the grass, and his back to a tree,
Merry as only a tinker can be,
  Busily tinkering, mending a pan,
  Singing as only a merry man can . . .
"Sym!" cried the riders. "'Tis thus you are styled?"
And he paused in his singing, and nodded and smiled.

Said he: "Last eve, when the sun was low,
Down thro' the bracken I watched her go—
  Down thro' the bracken, with simple grace—
  And the glory of eve shone full on her face;
And there on the sky-line it lingered a span,
So loth to be leaving my Emily Ann."

With hands to their faces the riders smiled.
"Sym," they said—"be it so you're styled—
  Behold, great Splosh, our sorrowing King,
  Has sent us hither, that we may bring
To the palace in Gosh a Glug so named,
That he may be honoured and justly famed."

"Yet," said Sym, as he tinkered his can,
"What should you know of her, Emily Ann?
  Early as cock-crow yester morn
  I watched young sunbeams, newly born,
As out of the East they frolicked and ran,
Eager to greet her, my Emily Ann."

"King Splosh," said the riders, "is bowed with grief;
And the glory of Gosh is a yellowing leaf.
    Up with you, Tinker! There's work ahead,
    With a King forsaken, and Swanks in dread,
To whom may we turn for the salving of man?"
And Sym, he answered them, "Emily Ann."

Said he: "Whenever I watch her pass,
With her skirts so high o'er the dew-wet grass,
    I envy every blade the bruise
    It earns in the cause of her twinkling shoes.
Oh, the dew-wet grass, where this morn she ran,
Was doubly jewelled for Emily Ann."

"But haste!" they cried. "By the palace gates
A sorrowing king for a tinker waits.
    And what shall we answer our Lord the King
    If never a tinker hence we bring,
To tinker a kingdom so sore amiss?"
But Sym, he said to them, "Answer him this:

'Every eve, when the clock chimes eight,
I kiss her fair, by her mother's gate:
    Twice, all reverent, on the brow—
    Once for a pray'r, and once for a vow;
Twice on her eyes that they may shine,
Then, full on the mouth because she's mine.' "

"Calf!" sneered the riders. "O Tinker, heed!
Mount and away with us, we must speed.
    All Gosh is agog for the coming of Sym.
    Garlands and greatness are waiting for him:
Garlands of roses, and garments of red,
And a chaplet for crowning a conqueror's head.

"Listen," quoth Sym, as he stirred his fire.
"Once in my life have I known desire.
    Then, Oh, but the touch of her kindled a flame
    That burns as a sun by the candle of fame.
And a blessing and boon for a poor tinker man
Looks out from the eyes of my Emily Ann."

Then they said to him, "Fool! Do you cast aside
Promise of honour, and place, and pride,
  Gold for the asking, and power o'er men—
  Working your will with the stroke of a pen?
Vexed were the King if you ride not with us."
But Sym, he said to them, "Answer him thus:

'Ease and honour and leave to live—
These are the gifts that a king may give . . . '
  'Twas over the meadow I saw her first;
  And my lips grew parched like a man athirst.
Oh, my treasure was ne'er in the gift of man;
For the gods have given me Emily Ann."

"Listen," said they, "O you crazy Sym.
Roses perish, and eyes grow dim.
  Lustre fades from the fairest hair.
  Who weds a woman links arms with care.
But women there are in the city of Gosh—
Ay, even the daughters of good King Splosh . . ."

"Care," said Sym, "is a weed that springs
Even to-day in the garden of kings.
  And I, who have lived 'neath the tent of the skies,
  Know of the flowers, and which to prize . . .
Give you good even! For now I must jog."
And he whistled him once to his little red dog.

Into the meadow and over the stile,
Off went the tinker man, singing the while;
  Down by the bracken patch, over the hill,
  With the little red dog at the heel of him still.
And back, as he soberly sauntered along,
There came to the riders the tail of his song:

"Kettles and pans! Kettles and pans!
Strong is my arm if the cause it be man's.
  But a fig for the cause of a cunning old king;
  For Emily Ann will be mine in the Spring.
Then naught shall I labour for Splosh or his plans;
Tho' I'll mend him a kettle. Ho, kettles and pans!"

THE LITTLE RED DOG

THE Glugs still live in the land of Gosh,
Under the rule of the great King Splosh;
  And they climb the trees in the Summer and Spring,
  Because it is reckoned the regular thing.
Down in the Valley they live their lives,
Taking the air with their aunts and wives.
  And they climb the trees in the Winter and Fall,
  And count it improper to climb not at all.

And they name their trees with a thousand names,
Calling them after their Arts and Aims;
  And some, they climb for the fun of the thing,
  But most go up at the call of the King.
Some scale a tree that they fear to name,
For it bears great blossoms of scarlet shame.
  But they eat of the fruit of the nameless tree,
  Because they are Glugs, and their choice is free.

But every eve, when the sun goes West,
Over the mountain they call The Blest,
  Whose summit looks down on the city of Gosh,
  Far from the reach of the great King Splosh,
The Glugs gaze up at the heights above,
And feel vague promptings to wondrous love.
  And they whisper a tale of a tinker man,
  Who lives in the mount with his Emi'y Ann.

A great mother mountain, and kindly is she,
Who nurses young rivers and sends them to sea.
  And, nestled high up on her sheltering lap,
  Is a little red house with a little straw cap
That bears a blue feather of smoke, curling high,
And a bunch of red roses cocked over one eye.
  And the eyes of it glisten and shine in the sun,
  As they look down on Gosh with a twinkle of fun.

There's a gay little garden, a tidy white gate,
And a narrow brown pathway that will not run straight;
  For it turns and it twists and it wanders about
  To the left and the right, as in humorous doubt.
'Tis a humorous path, and a joke from its birth
Till it ends at the door with a wriggle of mirth.
  And here in the mount lives the queer tinker man
  With his little red dog and his Emily Ann.

And, once in a while, when the weather is clear,
When the work is all over, and even is near,
  They walk in the garden and gaze down below
  On the Valley of Gosh, where the young rivers go;
Where the houses of Gosh seem so paltry and vain,
Like a handful of pebbles strewn over the plain;
  Where tiny black forms crawl about in the vale,
  And stare at the mountain they fear them to scale.

And Sym sits him down by his little wife's knee,
With his feet in the grass and his back to a tree;
  And he looks on the Valley and dreams of old years,
  As he strokes his red dog with the funny prick ears.
And he says, "Still they climb in their whimsical way,
While we stand on earth, yet are higher than they.
  Oh, who trusts to a tree is a fool of a man!
  For the wise seek the mountains, my Emily Ann."

So lives the queer tinker, nor deems it a wrong,
When the spirit so moves him, to burst into song.
  'Tis a comical song about kettles and pans,
  And the graces and charms that are Emily Ann's.
'Tis a mad, freakish song, but he sings it with zest,
And his little wife vows it of all songs the best.
  And he sings quite a lot, as the Summer days pass,
  With his back to a tree and his feet in the grass.

And the little red dog, who is wise as dogs go,
He will hark to that song for a minute or so,
  With his head on one side, and a serious air.
  Then he makes no remark; but he wanders elsewhere.

And he trots down the garden to gaze now and then
At the curious pranks of a certain blue wren:
   Not a commonplace wren, but a bird marked for fame
   Thro' a grievance in life and a definite aim.

Now, they never fly far and they never fly high,
And they probably couldn't, suppose they should try.
   So the common blue wren is content with his lot:
   He will eat when there's food, and he fasts when there's not.
He flirts and he flutters, his wife by his side,
With his share of content and forgiveable pride.
   And he keeps to the earth, 'mid the bushes and shrubs,
   And he dines very well upon corpulent grubs.

But the little blue wren with a grievance in life,
He was rude to his neighbours and short with his wife.
   For, up in the apple-tree over his nest,
   There dwelt a fat spider who gave him no rest:
A spider so fat, so abnormally stout
That he seemed hardly fitted to waddle about.
   But his eyes were so sharp, and his legs were so spry,
   That he could not be caught; and 'twas folly to try.

Said the wren, as his loud lamentations he hurled
At the little red dog, "It's a rotten old world!
   But my heart would be glad, and my life would be blest
   If I had that fat spider well under my vest.
Then I'd call back my youth, and be seeking to live,
And to taste of the pleasures the world has to give.
   But the world is all wrong, and my mind's in a fog!"
   "Aw, don't be a Glug!" said the little red dog.

Then, up from the grass, where he sat by his tree,
The voice of the Tinker rose fearless and free.

The little dog listened, his head on one side;
Then sought him a spot where a bored dog could hide.

"Kettles and pans! Ho, kettles and pans!
The stars are the gods' but the earth, it is man's!
   Yet down in the shadow dull mortals there are
   Who climb in the tree-tops to snatch at a star:
Seeking content and a surcease of care,
Finding but emptiness everywhere.
   Then make for the mountain, importunate man!
   With a kettle to mend . . . and your Emily Ann."

As he cocked a sad eye o'er a sheltering log,
"Oh, a Glug *is* a Glug!" sighed the little red dog.

ROUNDABOUT

[*With his nimble fancy, feeling for decorative language, and remarkable rhyming agility, Dennis was as well equipped for the writing of child verses as for the production of bush ballads and verse-tales of the lives of larrikins. In addition, his versatility became emphasized when he illustrated his volume for youth, which contains both prose and verse, with quaint little sketches of his own making. The book first appeared in 1921 as* A Book for Kids *and was issued again in 1935 under the title of* Roundabout. *Many of the verses are delightful. Dennis himself expressed a preference for "The Swagman". Another poet chose "The Ant Explorer". It is hoped that most other favourites have been included in the present choice.*]

CUPPACUMALONGA

"Rover, rover, cattle-drover, where go you to-day?"
I go to Cuppacumalonga, fifty miles away;
  Over plains where Summer rains have sung a song of glee,
  Over hills where laughing rills go seeking for the sea,
I go to Cuppacumalonga, to my brother Bill.
    Then come along, ah, come along!
      Ah, come to Cuppacumalonga!
        Come to Cuppacumalonga Hill!

"Rover, rover, cattle-drover, how do you get there?"
For twenty miles I amble on upon my pony mare,
  Then walk awhile and talk awhile to country men I know,
  Then up to ride a mile beside a team that travels slow,
And last to Cuppacumalonga, riding with a will.
    Then come along, ah, come along!
      Ah, come to Cuppacumalonga!
        Come to Cuppacumalonga Hill!

"Rover, rover, cattle-drover, what do you do then?"
I camp beneath a kurrajong with three good cattle-men;
  Then off away at break of day, with strong hands on the reins,
  To laugh and sing while mustering the cattle on the plains—
For up at Cuppacumalonga life is jolly still.
    Then come along, ah, come along!
      Ah, come to Cuppacumalonga!
        Come to Cuppacumalonga Hill!

"Rover, rover, cattle-drover, how may I go too?"
I'll saddle up my creamy colt and he shall carry you—
  My creamy colt who will not bolt, who does not shy nor kick—
  We'll pack the load and take the road and travel very quick.
And if the day brings work or play we'll meet it with a will.
    So Hi for Cuppacumalonga!
      Come along, ah, come along!
        Ah, come to Cuppacumalonga Hill!

THE ANT EXPLORER

ONCE a little sugar ant made up his mind to roam—
To fare away far away, far away from home.
He had eaten all his breakfast, and he had his ma's consent
To see what he should chance to see and here's the way he went—
Up and down a fern frond, round and round a stone,
Down a gloomy gully where he loathed to be alone,
Up a mighty mountain range, seven inches high,
Through the fearful forest grass that nearly hid the sky,
Out along a bracken bridge, bending in the moss,
Till he reached a dreadful desert that was feet and feet across.
'Twas a dry, deserted desert, and a trackless land to tread;
He wished that he was home again and tucked-up tight in bed.
His little legs were wobbly, his strength was nearly spent,
And so he turned around again and here's the way he went—
Back away from desert lands feet and feet across,
Back along the bracken bridge bending in the moss,
Through the fearful forest grass shutting out the sky,
Up a mighty mountain range seven inches high,
Down a gloomy gully, where he loathed to be alone,
Up and down a fern frond and round and round a stone.
A dreary ant, a weary ant, resolved no more to roam,
He staggered up the garden path and popped back home.

THE SWAGMAN

OH, he was old and he was spare;
His bushy whiskers and his hair
Were all fussed up and very grey;
He said he'd come a long, long way
And had a long, long way to go.
Each boot was broken at the toe,
And he'd a swag upon his back.
His billy-can, as black as black,
Was just the thing for making tea
At picnics, so it seemed to me.

'Twas hard to earn a bite of bread,
He told me. Then he shook his head,
And all the little corks that hung
Around his hat-brim danced and swung
And bobbed about his face; and when
I laughed he made them dance again.
He said they were for keeping flies—
"The pesky varmints"—from his eyes.
He called me "Codger" . . . "Now you see
The best days of your life," said he.
"But days will come to bend your back,
And, when they come, keep off the track.
Keep off, young codger, if you can."
He seemed a funny sort of man.

He told me that he wanted work,
But jobs were scarce this side of Bourke,
And he supposed he'd have to go
Another fifty mile or so.
"Nigh all my life the track I've walked,"
He said. I liked the way he talked.
And oh, the places he had seen!
I don't know where he had not been—

On every road, in every town,
All through the country, up and down.
"Young codger, shun the track," he said.
And put his hand upon my head.
I noticed, then, that his old eyes
Were very blue and very wise.
"Ay, once I was a little lad,"
He said, and seemed to grow quite sad.

I sometimes think: When I'm a man,
I'll get a good black billy-can
And hang some corks around my hat,
And lead a jolly life like that.

THE POSTMAN

I'D like to be a postman, and walk along the street,
  Calling out, "Good Morning, Sir," to gentlemen I meet;
Ringing every door-bell all along my beat,
In my cap and uniform so very nice and neat.
Perhaps I'd have a parasol in case of rain or heat;
    But I wouldn't be a postman if . . . .
      The walking hurt my feet.
        Would you?

THE TRAVELLER

As I rode in to Burrumbeet,
I met a man with funny feet;
And, when I paused to ask him why
His feet were strange, he rolled his eye
And said the rain would spoil the wheat;
So I rode on to Burrumbeet.

As I rode in to Beetaloo,
I met a man whose nose was blue;
And when I asked him how he got
A nose like that, he answered, "What
Do bullocks mean when they say 'Moo'?"
So I rode on to Beetaloo.

As I rode in to Ballarat,
I met a man who wore no hat;
And, when I said he might take cold,
He cried, "The hills are quite as old
As yonder plains, but not so flat."
So I rode on to Ballarat.

As I rode in to Gundagai,
I met a man and passed him by
Without a nod, without a word.
He turned, and said he'd never heard
Or seen a man so wise as I.
But I rode on to Gundagai.

As I rode homeward, full of doubt,
I met a stranger riding out:
A foolish man he seemed to me;
But, "Nay, I am yourself," said he,
"Just as you were when you rode out."
So I rode homeward, free of doubt.

THE TRIANTIWONTIGONGOLOPE

THERE'S a very funny insect that you do not often spy,
And it isn't quite a spider, and it isn't quite a fly;
It is something like a beetle, and a little like a bee,
But nothing like a woolly grub that climbs upon a tree.
Its name is quite a hard one, but you'll learn it soon, I hope.
So, try:

    Tri-
        Tri-anti-wonti-
            Triantiwontigongolope.

It lives on weeds and wattle-gum, and has a funny face;
Its appetite is hearty, and its manners a disgrace.
When first you come upon it, it will give you quite a scare,
But when you look for it again you find it isn't there.
And unless you call it softly it will stay away and mope.
So, try:

    Tri-
        Tri-anti-wonti-
            Triantiwontigongolope.

It trembles if you tickle it or tread upon its toes;
It is not an early riser, but it has a snubbish nose
If you sneer at it, or scold it, it will scuttle off in shame,
But it purrs and purrs quite proudly if you call it by its name,
And offer it some sandwiches of sealing-wax and soap.
So, try:

    Tri-
        Tri-anti-wonti-
            Triantiwontigongolope.

O

But of course you haven't seen it; and I truthfully confess
That I haven't seen it either, and I don't know its address.
For there isn't such an insect, though there really might have been
If the trees and grass were purple, and the sky was bottle-green.
It's just a little joke of mine, which you'll forgive, I hope.
Oh, try!

    Try!

      Tri-anti-wonti-

        Triantiwontigongolope.

THE CIRCUS

Hey, there! Hoop-la! the circus is in town!
Have you seen the elephant? Have you seen the clown?
Have you seen the dappled horse gallop round the ring?
Have you seen the acrobats on the dizzy swing?
Have you seen the tumbling men tumble up and down?
Hoop-la! Hoop-la! the circus is in town!

Hey, there! Hoop-la! Here's the circus troupe!
Here's the educated dog jumping through the hoop.
See the lady Blondin with the parasol and fan,
The lad upon the ladder and the india-rubber man.
See the joyful juggler and the boy who loops the loop.
Hey! Hey! Hey! Hey! Here's the circus troupe!

THE TRAM-MAN

I'D like to be a Tram-man, and ride about all day,
Calling out, "Fares, please!" in quite a 'ficious way,
With pockets full of pennies which I'd make the people pay.
But in the hottest days I'd take my tram down to the Bay;
And when I saw the nice cool sea I'd shout "Hip, hip, hooray!"
    But I wouldn't be a tram-man if . . . .
        I couldn't stop and play.
                Would you?

GOING TO SCHOOL

Did you see them pass to-day, Billy, Kate and Robin,
All astride upon the back of old grey Dobbin?
Jigging, jogging off to school, down the dusty track—
What must Dobbin think of it—three upon his back?
Robin at the bridle-rein, in the middle Kate,
Billy holding on behind, his legs out straight.

Now they're coming back from school, jig, jog, jig.
See them at the corner where the gums grow big;
Dobbin flicking off the flies and blinking at the sun—
Having three upon his back he thinks is splendid fun:
Robin at the bridle-rein, in the middle Kate,
Little Billy up behind, his legs out straight.

BACKBLOCK BALLADS

[*Published in 1918,* Backblock Ballads and Later Verses *reprints some of the material in Dennis's first book (1913) and adds other verses, together with illustrations by Hal Gye. As the later book contains thirty-seven items, ranging from bush ballads to "The Austra—laise" and "A Guide for Poits", it is impossible to give here a thorough representation of the work. Choice has been limited, therefore, to a few ballads and the prophetic "Hymn of Futility". This "hymn", like "The Nearing Drums", which appeared in the book of 1913, demonstrates the poet's awareness of the danger to Australia that became emphatically revealed in 1941.*]

AN OLD MASTER

WE were cartin' laths and palin's from the slopes of Mount St
    Leonard,
  With our axles near the road-bed and the mud as stiff as glue;
And our bullocks weren't precisely what you'd call conditioned
    nicely,
  And meself and Messmate Mitchell had our doubts of gettin'
    through.

It had rained a tidy skyful in the week before we started,
  But our tucker-bag depended on the sellin' of our load;
So we punched 'em on by inches, liftin' 'em across the pinches,
  Till we struck the final section of the worst part of the road.

We were just congratulatin' one another on the goin',
  When we blundered in a pot-hole right within the sight of goal,
Where the bush-track joins the metal. Mitchell, as he saw her settle,
  Justified his reputation at the peril of his soul.

We were 'n a glue-pot, certain—red and stiff and most tenacious;
  Over naves and over axles—waggon sittin' on the road.
"'Struth," says I, "they'll never lift her. Take a shot from Hell to
    shift her.
  Nothin' left but to unyoke 'em and sling off the blessed load."

Now, beside our scene of trouble stood a little one-roomed humpy,
  Home of an enfeebled party by the name of Dad McGee.
Daddy was, I pause to mention, livin' on an old-age pension
  Since he gave up bullock-punchin' at the age of eighty-three.

Startled by our exclamations, Daddy hobbled from the shanty,
  Gazin' where the stranded waggon looked like some half-
    foundered ship.
When the state o' things he spotted, "Looks," he says, "like you was
    potted,"
  And he toddles up to Mitchell. "Here," says he, "gimme that
    whip."

Well! I've heard of transformations; heard of fellers sort of changin'
  In the face of sudden danger or some great emergency;
Heard the like in song and story and in bush traditions hoary,
  But I nearly dropped me bundle as I looked at Dad McGee.

While we gazed he seemed to toughen; as his fingers gripped the handle
  His old form grew straight and supple, and a light leapt in his eye;
And he stepped around the waggon, not with footsteps weak and laggin',
  But with firm, determined bearin', as he flung the whip on high.

Now he swung the leaders over, while the whip-lash snarled and volleyed;
  And they answered like one bullock, strainin' to each crack and clout;
But he kept his cursin' under till old Brindle made a blunder;
  Then I thought all Hell had hit me, *and the master opened out.*

And the language! Oh, the language! Seemed to me I must be dreamin';
  While the wondrous words and phrases only genius could produce
Roared and rumbled, fast and faster, in the throat of that Old Master—
  Oaths and curses tipped with lightning, cracklin' flames of fierce abuse.

Then we knew the man before us was a Master of our callin';
  One of those great lords of language gone for ever from Outback;
Heroes of an ancient order; men who punched across the border;
  Vanished giants of the sixties; puncher-princes of the track.

Now we heard the timbers strainin', heard the waggon's loud complainin',
  And the master cried triumphant, as he swung 'em into line,
As they put their shoulders to it, lifted her, and pulled her through it:
  "That's the way we useter do it in the days o' sixty-nine!"

Near the foot of Mount St Leonard lives an old, enfeebled party
  Who retired from bullock-punchin' at the age of eighty-three.
If you seek him folk will mention, merely, that he draws the pension;
  But to us he looms a Master—Prince of Punchers, Dad McGee!

WHEAT

"Sowin' things an' growin' things, an' watchin' of 'em grow;
That's the game," my father said, an' father ought to know.
"Settin' things an' gettin' things to grow for folks to eat:
That's the life," my father said, "that's very hard to beat."
For my father was a farmer, as his father was before,
Just sowin' things an' growin' things in far-off days of yore,
In the far-off land of England, till my father found his feet
In the new land, in the true land, where he took to growin' wheat.
  Wheat, Wheat, Wheat! Oh, the sound of it is sweet!
  I've been praisin' it an' raisin' it in rain an' wind an' heat
    Since the time I learned to toddle, till it's beatin' in my noddle,
  Is the little song I'm singin' you of Wheat, Wheat, Wheat.

Plantin' things—an' grantin' things is goin' as they should,
An' the weather altogether is behavin' pretty good—
Is a pleasure in a measure for a man that likes the game,
An' my father he would rather raise a crop than make a name.
For my father was a farmer, an' "All fame," he said, "ain't reel;
An' the same it isn't fillin' when you're wantin' for a meal."
So I'm followin' his footsteps, an' a-keepin' of my feet,
While I cater for the nation with my Wheat, Wheat, Wheat.
  Wheat, Wheat, Wheat! When the poets all are beat
  By the reason that the season for the verse crop is a cheat,
    Then I comes up bright an' grinnin' with the knowledge that
      I'm winnin',
  With the rhythm of my harvester an' Wheat, Wheat, Wheat.

Readin' things an' heedin' things that clever fellers give,
An' ponderin' an' wonderin' why we was meant to live—
Muddlin' through an' fuddlin' through philosophy an' such
Is a game I never took to, an' it doesn't matter much.
For my father was a farmer, as I might 'a' said before,
An' the sum of his philosophy was, "Grow a little more.
For growin' things," my father said, "it makes life sort o' sweet
An' your conscience never swats you if your game is growin' wheat."

Wheat, Wheat, Wheat! Oh, the people have to eat!
An' you're servin', an' deservin' of a velvet-cushion seat
* In the cocky-farmers' heaven when you come to throw a seven;*
An' your password at the portal will be, "Wheat, Wheat, Wheat."

In the city, more's the pity, thousands live an' thousands die
Never carin', never sparin' pains that fruits may multiply;
Breathin', livin', never givin'; greedy but to have an' take,
Dyin' with no day behind 'em lived for fellow-mortals' sake.
Now my father was a farmer, an' he used to sit and laugh
At the "fools o' life", he called 'em, livin' on the other half.
Dyin' lonely, missin' only that one joy that makes life sweet—
Just the joy of useful labour, such as comes of growin' wheat.
* Wheat, Wheat, Wheat! Let the foolish scheme an' cheat;*
* But I'd rather, like my father, when my span o' life's complete,*
*   Feel I'd lived by helpin' others; earned the right to call 'em*
*   brothers*
* Who had gained while I was gainin' from God's earth His gift*
*   of wheat.*

When the settin' sun is gettin' low above the western hills,
When the creepin' shadows deepen, and a peace the whole land fills,
Then I often sort o' soften with a feelin' like content,
An' I feel like thankin' Heaven for a day in labour spent.
For my father was a farmer, an' he used to sit an' smile,
Realizin' he was wealthy in what makes a life worth while.
Smilin', he has told me often, "After all the toil an' heat,
Lad, he's paid in more than silver who has grown one field of
    wheat."
* Wheat, Wheat, Wheat! When it comes my turn to meet*
* Death the Reaper, an' the Keeper of the Judgment Book I greet,*
*   Then I'll face 'em sort o' calmer with the solace of the farmer*
* That he's fed a million brothers with his Wheat, Wheat,*
*   Wheat.*

'URRY!

Now, *Ma-til-der*! Ain't cher dressed yet? I declare, the girl ain't up!
Last as ushul. Move yerself, you sleepy-'ead!
Are you goin' to lie there lazin',
W'ile I—Nell, put down that basin;
Go an' see if Bill has got the poddies fed;
Tell 'im not to move that clucky—ho, yer up, me lady, eh?
That's wot comes from gallivantin' late ut night.
Why, the sun is nearly—see now,
Don't chu *dare* talk back at me now!
Set the table, Nell! Where's Nell? Put out that light!

Now then, 'urry, goodness, 'urry! *Mary*, tell the men to come.
Oh there, drat the girl! MA-TIL-DER! *where's the jam?*
You fergot it? Well, uv all ther . . . .
Mary! 'Ear me tell you call ther . . . .
Lord! *there's Baldy* TANGLED IN THE BARB'-WIRE—SAM!
Now, then, take 'er steady, clumsy, or she'll cut herself—LEAVE
    OFF!
Do you want the cow to—*There!* I never did!
Well, you mighter took 'er steady.
Sit up, Dad, yer late already.
Did ju put the tea in, Mary? Where's the lid?

Oh, do 'urry! Where's them buckets? *Nell*, 'as Bill brought in the
    cows?
Where's that boy? Ain't finished eatin' yet, uv course;
Eat all day if 'e wus let to.
Mary, where'd yer father get to?
Gone! Wot! *Call 'im back!* DAD! Wot about that 'orse?
No, indeed, it ain't my business; you kin see the man yerself.
No, I *won't*! I'm sure I've quite enough to do.
If 'e calls ter-day about it,
'E kin either go without it,
Or elst walk acrost the paddick out to you.

Are the cows in, *B-i-ll*? Oh, there they are. Well, nearly time they—
 Nell,
Feed the calves, an' pack the—*Yes, indeed ju will!*
Get the sepy-rater ready.
Woa, there, Baldy—steady, *steady.*
Bail up. *Stop-er! Hi, Matilder!* MARY! BILL!
Well, uv all th' . . . . *Now* you've done it.
Wait till Dad comes 'ome to-night;
When 'e sees the mess you've—*Don't stand starin' there!*
Go an' get the cart an' neddy;
An' the cream cans—are they ready?
Where's the . . . . There! Fergot the fowls, I *do* declare!

Chuck!—*Chook!*—CHOOK! Why, there's that white un lost
 another chick to-day!
Nell, 'ow many did I count?—*Oh, stop that row!*
Wot's 'e doin'? Oh, you daisy!
Do you mean to tell me, lazy,
Thet you 'aven't fed the pigs until jus' now?
Oh, *do 'urry!* There's the men ull soon be knockin' off fer lunch.
An' we 'aven't got the . . . . Reach that bacon down.
Get the billies, Nell, an'—*Mary,*
Go an' fetch the . . . . Wot? *'Ow dare 'e!*
Bill, yer NOT *to wear yer best 'at inter town!*

'Ave you washed the things, Matilder? Oh, do 'urry, girl, yer late!
Seems to me you trouble more—TAKE CARE!—*You dunce!*
Now you've broke it! Well I never!
Ain't chu mighty smart an' clever;
Try'n to carry arf a dozen things at once.
No back answers now! You hussy! Don't chu *dare* talk back at me
Or I'll . . . Nelly, did ju give them eggs to Bill?
Wot? CHU NEVER? Well I . . . . Mary,
Bring them dishes frum the dairy;
No, not them, the . . . . Lord, the sun's be'ind the hill!

'Ave you cleaned the sepy-rater, Nell? Well, get along to bed.
No; you can't go 'crost to Thompson's place to-night;
You wus there las' Chusday—See, miss,
Don't chu toss your head at *me*, miss!
I won't 'ave it. Mary, *'urry* with that light!
Now then, get yer Dad the paper. Set down, Dad—ju must be tired.
'Ere, Matilder, put that almanick away!
Where's them stockin's I wus·darnin'?
Bill an' Mary, stop yer yarnin'!
Now then, Dad. Heigh-ho! Me fust sit down ter-day.

THE SILENT MEMBER

He lived in Mundaloo, and Bill McClosky was his name,
But folks that knew him well had little knowledge of that same;
For he some'ow lost his surname, and he had so much to say—
He was called "The Silent Member" in a mild, sarcastic way.

He could talk on any subject—from the weather and the crops
To astronomy and Euclid, and he never minded stops;
And the lack of a companion didn't lay him on the shelf,
For he'd stand before a looking-glass and argue with himself.

He would talk for hours on lit'rature, or calves, or art, or wheat;
There was not a bally subject you could say had got him beat;
And when strangers brought up topics that they reckoned he would
    baulk,
He'd remark, "I never heard of that." But all the same—he'd talk.

He'd talk at christ'nings by the yard; at weddings by the mile;
And he used to pride himself upon his choice of words and style.
In a funeral procession his remarks would never end
On the qualities and virtues of the dear departed friend.

We got quite used to hearing him, and no one seemed to care—
In fact, no happ'ning seemed complete unless his voice was there.
For close on thirty year he talked, and none could talk him down,
Until one day an agent for insurance struck the town.

Well, we knew The Silent Member, and we knew what he could do,
And it wasn't very long before we knew the agent, too,
As a crack long-distance talker that was pretty hard to catch;
So we called a hasty meeting and decided on a match.

Of course, we didn't tell them we were putting up the game;
But we fixed it up between us, and made bets upon the same.
We named a time-keep and a referee to see it through;
Then strolled around, just casual, and introduced the two.

The agent got first off the mark, while our man stood and grinned;
He talked for just one solid hour, then stopped to get his wind.
"Yes; but—" sez Bill; that's all he said; he couldn't say no more;
The agent got right in again, and fairly held the floor.

On policies, and bonuses, and premiums, and all that,
He talked and talked until we thought he had our man out flat.
"I think—" Bill got in edgeways, but that there insurance chap
Just filled himself with atmosphere, and took the second lap.

I saw our man was getting dazed, and sort of hypnotized,
And they oughter pulled the agent up right there, as I advised.
"See here—" Bill started, husky; but the agent came again,
And talked right on for four hours good—from six o'clock to ten.

Then Bill began to crumple up, and weaken at the knees,
When all at once he ups and shouts, "Here, give a bloke a breeze!
Just take a pull for half a tick and let me have the floor,
And I'll take out a policy." The agent said no more.

The Silent Member swallowed hard, then coughed and cleared his
    throat,
But not a single word would come—no; not a blessed note.
His face looked something dreadful—such a look of pained dismay;
Then he gave us one pathetic glance, and turned, and walked away.

He's hardly spoken since that day—not more than "Yes" or "No".
We miss his voice a good bit, too; the town seems rather slow.
He was called "The Silent Member" just sarcastic, I'll allow;
But since that agent handled him it sort o' fits him now.

P

THE BRIDGE ACROSS THE CRICK

JOSEPH Jones and Peter Dawking
    Strove in an election fight;
And you'd think, to hear them talking,
    Each upheld the people's right.
Each declared he stood for Progress and against his country's foes
When he sought their votes at Wombat, where the Muddy River
      flows.

Peter Dawking, scorning party,
    As an Independent ran;
Joseph Jones, loud, blatant, hearty,
    Was a solid party man.
But the electors up at Wombat vowed to him alone they'd stick
Who would give his sacred promise for the "bridge across the crick".

Bland, unfaithful politicians
    Long had said this bridge should be.
Some soared on to high positions,
    Some sank to obscurity;
Still the bridge had been denied it by its unrelenting foes—
By the foes of patient Wombat, where the Muddy River flows.

Up at Wombat Peter Dawking
    Held a meeting in the hall,
And he'd spent an hour in talking
    On the far-flung Empire's Call,
When a local greybeard, rising, smote him with this verbal brick:
"Are or are yeh not in favour of the bridge across the crick?"

Peter just ignored the question,
    Proudly patriotic man;
Understand a mean suggestion
    Men like Peter never can,
Or that free enlightened voters look on all Great Things as rot,
While a Burning Local Question fires each local patriot.

Joseph Jones, serene and smiling,
    Took all Wombat to his heart.
"Ah," he said, his "blood was b'iling"—
    He declared it "made him smart"
To reflect how they'd been swindled; and he cried in ringing tones
"Gentlemen, your bridge is certain if you cast your votes for Jones!"

Joseph Jones and Peter Dawking
    Strove in an election fight,
And, when they had finished talking,
    On the great election night
They stood level in the voting, and the hope of friends and foes
Hung upon the box from Wombat, where the Muddy River flows.

Then the Wombat votes were counted;
    Jones, two hundred; Dawking, three!
Joseph, proud and smiling, mounted
    On a public balcony,
And his friends were shrill with triumph, for that contest, shrewdly
        run,
In the House gave Jones's Party a majority of one.

Jones's Party—note the sequel—
    Rules that country of the Free,
And the fight, so nearly equal,
    Swayed the whole land's destiny.
And the Big Things of the Nation are delayed till Hope grows sick—
Offered up as sacrifices to "the bridge across the crick".

Dawking now is sadly fearing
    For the crowd's intelligence.
Joseph, skilled in engineering,
    Full of pomp and sly pretence,
Still holds out the pleasing promise of that bridge whene'er he goes
Up to Wombat, patient Wombat, where the Muddy River flows.

A SONG OF RAIN

BECAUSE a little vagrant wind veered south from China Sea;
Or else, because a sun-spot stirred; and yet again, maybe
Because some idle god in play breathed on an errant cloud,
The heads of twice two million folk in gratitude are bowed.

> *Patter, patter . . . Boolcoomatta,*
> *Adelaide and Oodnadatta,*
> *Pepegoona, parched and dry*
> *Laugh beneath a dripping sky.*
> *Riverina's thirsting plain*
> *Knows the benison of rain.*
> *Ararat and Arkaroola*
> *Render thanks with Tantanoola*
> *For the blessings they are gaining,*
> *And it's raining—raining—raining!*

Because a heav'n-sent monsoon the mists before it drove;
Because things happened in the moon; or else, because High Jove,
Unbending, played at waterman to please a laughing boy,
The hearts through all a continent are raised in grateful joy

> *Weeps the sky at Wipipee*
> *Far Farina's folk are dippy*
> *With sheer joy, while Ballarat*
> *Shouts and flings aloft its hat.*
> *Thirsty Thackaringa yells;*
> *Taltabooka gladly tells*
> *Of a season wet and windy;*
> *Men rejoice on Murrindindie;*
> *Kalioota's ceased complaining;*
> *For it's raining—raining—raining!*

Because a poor bush parson prayed an altruistic prayer,
Rich with unselfish fellow-love that Heaven counted rare;
And yet, mayhap, because one night a meteor was hurled
Across the everlasting blue, the luck was with our world.

On the wilds of Winininnie
Cattle low and horses whinny,
Frolicking with sheer delight.
From Beltana to The Bight,
In the Mallee's sun-scorched towns,
In the sheds on Darling Downs,
In the huts at Yudnapinna,
Tents on Tidnacoordininna,
To the sky all heads are craning—
For it's raining—raining—raining!

Because some strange, cyclonic thing has happened—God knows
    where—
Men dream again of easy days, of cash to spend and spare.
The ring fair Clara coveted, Belinda's furs are nigh,
As clerklings watch their increments fall shining from the sky.

Rolls the thunder at Eudunda;
Leongatha, Boort, Kapunda
Send a joyous message down;
Sorrows, flooded, sink and drown.
Ninkerloo and Nerim South
Hail the breaking of the drouth;
From Toolangi's wooded mountains
Sounds the song of plashing fountains;
Sovereign Summer's might is waning;
It is raining—raining—raining!

Because the breeze blew sou'-by-east across the China Sea;
Or else, because the thing was willed through all eternity
By gods that rule the rushing stars, or gods long aeons dead,
The earth is made to smile again, and living things are fed.

Mile on mile from Mallacoota
Runs the news, and far Baroota
Speeds it over hill and plain,
Till the slogan of the rain
Rolls afar to Yankalilla;
Wallaroo and Wirrawilla
Shout it o'er the leagues between,

Telling of the dawning green.
Frogs at Cocoroc are croaking,
Booboorowie soil is soaking,
Oodla Wirra, Orroroo
Breathe relief and hope anew.
Wycheproof and Wollongong
Catch the burden of the song
That is rolling, rolling ever
O'er the plains of Never Never,
Sounding in each mountain rill,
Echoing from hill to hill . . .
In the lonely, silent places
Men lift up their glad, wet faces,
And their thanks ask no explaining—
It is raining—raining—raining!

HYMN OF FUTILITY

LORD, Thou hast given unto us a land.
  In Thy beneficence Thou has ordained
That we should hold a country great and grand,
  Such as no race of old has ever gained.
A favoured people, basking in Thy smile:
  So dost Thou leave us to work out our fate;
But, Lord, be patient yet a little while.
  The shade is pleasing and our task is great.

Lo, Thou hast said: "This land I give to you
  To be the cradle of a mighty race,
Who shall take up the White Man's task anew,
  And all the nations of the world outpace.
No heritage for cowards or for slaves,
  Here is a mission for the brave, the strong.
Then see ye to it, lest dishonoured graves
  Bear witness that he tarried overlong."

Lo, Thou hast said: "When ye have toiled and tilled,
  When ye have borne the heat, and wisely sown,
And every corner of the vineyard filled
  With goodly growth, the land shall be your own.
Then shall your sons and your sons' sons rejoice.
  Then shall the race speak with a conqueror's mouth;
And all the world shall hearken to its voice,
  And heed the great White Nation of the South."

And Thou hast said: "This, striving, shall ye do.
  Be diligent to tend and guard the soil.
If this great heritage I trust to you
  Be worth the purchase of a meed of toil,
Then shall ye not, at call of game or mart,
  Forgo the labour of a single day.
They spurn the gift who treasure but a part.
  Guard ye the whole, lest all be cast away."

· · · · · ·

Great cities have we builded here, O Lord;
    And corn and kine full plenty for our need
We have; and doth the wondrous land afford
    Treasure beyond the wildest dreams of greed.
Even this tiny portion of Thy gift,
    One corner of our mighty continent,
Doth please us well. A voice in prayer we lift:
    "Lord, give us peace! For we are well content."

Lord, give us peace; for Thou has sent a sign:
    Smoke of a raider's ships athwart the sky!
Nay, suffer us to hold this gift of Thine!
    The burden, Lord! The burden—by and by!
The sun is hot, Lord, and the way is long!
    'Tis pleasant in this corner Thou has blest.
Leave us to tarry here with wine and song.
    Our little corner, Lord! Guard Thou the rest!

But yesterday our fathers hither came,
    Rovers and strangers on a foreign strand.
Must we, for their neglect, bear all the blame?
    Nay, Master, *we have come to love our land!*
But see, the task Thou givest us is great;
    The load is heavy and the way is long!
Hold Thou our enemy without the gate;
    When we have rested then shall we be strong.

Lord, Thou hast spoken . . . And, with hands to ears,
    We would shut out the thunder of Thy voice
That in the nightwatch wakes our sudden fears—
    "The day is here, and yours must be the choice.
Will ye be slaves and shun the task of men?
    Will ye be weak who may be brave and strong?"
We wave our banners boastfully, and then,
    Weakly we answer, "Lord, the way is long!"

"Time tarries not, but here ye tarry yet,
    The futile masters of a continent,
Guard ye the gift I gave? Do ye forget?"
    And still we answer, "Lord, we are content.

Fat have we grown upon this goodly soil,
    A little while be patient, Lord, and wait.
To-morrow and to-morrow will we toil.
    The shade is pleasing, Lord! Our task is great!"

But ever through the clamour of the mart,
    And ever on the playground through the cheers:
"He spurns the gift who guardeth but a part"—
    So doth the warning fall on heedless ears.
"Guard ye the treasure if the gift be meet"—
    (Loudly we call the odds, we cheer the play.)
"For he who fears the burden and the heat
    Shall glean the harvest of a squandered day."

THE SINGING GARDEN

[*Dennis had become very fond of the birds and the trees about "Arden", his home at Toolangi, and in 1935 he got together a large series of verses on the subject, together with various prose sketches, which had been published in the Melbourne Herald, and put them into a book entitled* The Singing Garden. *No fewer than fifty kinds of birds are enshrined in verse, and the method used is the anthropomorphic one of having them tell their own stories. The book, therefore, is not specially distinguished, but both the verse and prose are warm with sunlight. This was Dennis's last book. A quotation from its final poem appears on his tombstone.*]

GREEN WALLS

I LOVE all gum-trees well. But, best of all,
 I love the tough old warriors that tower
About these lawns, to make a great green wall
 And guard, like sentries, this exotic bower
 Of shrub and fern and flower.
These are my land's own sons, lean, straight and tall,
Where crimson parrots and grey gang-gangs call
 Thro' many a sunlit hour.

My friends, these grave old veterans, scarred and stern,
 Changeless throughout the changing seasons they.
But at their knees their tall sons lift and yearn—
 Slim spars and saplings—prone to sport and sway
 Like carefree boys at play;
Waxing in beauty when their young locks turn
To crimson, and, like beacon fires burn
 To deck Spring's holiday.

I think of Anzacs when the dusk comes down
 Upon the gums—of Anzacs tough and tall.
Guarding this gateway, Diggers strong and brown.
 And when, thro' Winter's thunderings, sounds their call,
 Like Anzacs, too, they fall . . . .
Their ranks grow thin upon the hill's high crown:
My sentinels! But, where those ramparts frown,
 Their stout sons mend the wall.

THE LYRETAIL

FAR in the forest depths I dwell,
  The master mimic of them all,
To pour from out my secret dell
  Echo of many a bushland call,
That over all the forest spills;
  Echo of many a birdland note,
When out about the timbered hills
Sounds all that borrowed lore that fills
  My magic throat.

I am the artist. Songs to me
  From all this gay green land are sped;
And when the wondrous canopy
  Of my great, fronded tail is spread—
A glorious veil, at even's hush—
  Above my head, I do my part;
Then wren and robin, finch and thrush—
All are re-echoed in a rush
  Of perfect art.

Here by my regal throne of state,
  To serve me for a swift retreat,
The little runways radiate;
  And when the tread of alien feet
Draws near I vanish: ever prone
  To quick alarm when aught offends
That secret ritual of the throne.
My songs are for my mate alone,
  And favoured friends.

I am the artist. None may find,
  In all the world, a match for me:
Rare feathered loveliness combined
  With such enchanting minstrelsy.
In a land vocal with gay song
  I choose whate'er I may require;
I wait, I listen all day long,
Then to the music of a throng
  I tune my lyre.

THE INDIAN MYNA

GIMME the town an' its clamour an' clutter;
　　I ain't very fond of the bush;
For my cobbers are coves of the gardens and gutter—
　　A tough metropolitan push.
I ain't never too keen on the countryfied life;
It's the hustle an' bustle for me an' me wife.

So I swagger an' strut an' I cuss an' I swagger;
　　I'm wise to the city's hard way.
A bit of a bloke an' a bit of a bragger;
　　I've always got plenty to say.
Learned thro' knockin' about since my people came out
From the land at the back of Bombay.

When out in the bush I am never a ranger;
　　There never ain't nothin' to see.
Besides, them bush birds got no time for a stranger;
　　So town an' the traffic for me.
I sleep in the gardens an' loaf in the street,
An' sling off all day at the fellers I meet.

An' I swagger an' scold an' strut an' I swagger,
　　An' pick up me fun where I can,
Or tell off me wife, who's a bit of a nagger,
　　Or scrap with the sparrers for scran.
A bonzer at bluffin', I give you my word,
For, between you an' me, I'm a pretty tough bird.

THE SATIN BOWER-BIRD

SPARE a bloom of blue, lady,
  To adorn a bower.
A violet will do, lady—
  Any azure flower.
Since we hold a dance to-day,
We would make our ball-room gay,
Where the scented grasses sway,
  And the tall trees tower.

Beautiful but shy, lady,
  Yesterday we came
Dropping from the sky, lady,
  Flecks of golden flame—
Golden flame and royal blue—
We have come to beg of you
Any scrap of heaven's hue
  For our dancing game.

Spare us but a leaf, lady,
  If our suit be spurned
We shall play the thief, lady,
  When your back is turned;
Ravishing your garden plot
Of the choicest you have got—
Pansy or forget-me-not—
  Counting it well earned.

Then, if some rare chance, lady,
  Later should befall.
And you gain a glance, lady,
  At our dancing hall,
You will find your blossoms there
'Mid our decorations where,
With a proud, patrician air,
  We hold the Bushland Ball.

DUSK

Now is the healing, quiet hour that fills
  This gay, green world with peace and grateful rest.
Where lately over opalescent hills
  The blood of slain Day reddened all the west,
  Now comes at Night's behest,
A glow that over all the forest spills,
As with the gold of promised daffodils.
  Of all hours this is best.

It is the time for thoughts of holy things,
  Of half-forgotten friends and one's own folk.
O'er all, the garden-scented sweetness clings
  To mingle with the wood fire's drifting smoke.
  A bull-frog's startled croak
Sounds from the gully where the last bird sings
His laggard vesper hymn, with folded wings;
  And Night spreads forth her cloak.

Keeping their vigil where the great range yearns,
  Like rigid sentries stand the wise old gums.
On blundering wings a night-moth wheels and turns
  And lumbers on, mingling its drowsy hums
  With that far roll of drums,
Where the swift creek goes tumbling midst the ferns . . .
Now, as the first star in the zenith burns,
  The dear, soft darkness comes.

GLOSSARY

Alley, to toss in the: To give up the ghost.

Also ran, The: On the turf, horses that fail to secure a leading place; hence, obscure persons, nonentities.

Ammer-lock (Hammer-lock): A favourite and effective hold in wrestling.

Ard Case (Hard Case): A shrewd or humorous person.

Aussie: Australia; an Australian.

'Ayseed (Hayseed): A rustic.

Back Chat: Impudent repartee.

Back and Fill: To vacillate; to shuffle.

Back the Barrer: To intervene without invitation.

Bag of Tricks: All one's belongings.

Barmy (Balmy): Foolish; silly.

Barrack: To take sides.

Beak: A magistrate. (Possibly from Anglo-Saxon, Beag—a magistrate.)

Beano: A feast.

Beans: Coins; money.

Beat: Puzzled; defeated

Beat, off the: Out of the usual routine.

Beat the band: To amaze.

Beef (to beef it out): To declaim vociferously.

Bellers: The lungs.

Biff: To smite.

Bint: Girl.

Bird, to give the: To treat with derision.

Blighty: London.

Bli'me: An oath with the fangs drawn.

Blind: Deception, "bluff".

Blob: A shapeless mass.

Block: The head. To lose or do in the block: To become flustered; excited; angry; to lose confidence. To keep the block: To remain calm; dispassionate.

Block, the: A fashionable city walk.

Bloke: A male adult of the genus homo.

Blubber, blub: To weep.

Bob: A shilling.

Bokays: Compliments, flattery.

Boko: The nose.

Bong-tong: Patrician (Fr. bon ton).

Bonzer, boshter, bosker: Adjectives expressing the superlative of excellence.

221

Boodle: Money; wealth.

Book: In whist, six tricks.

Book: A bookie, q.v.

Booked: Engaged.

Bookie: A book-maker (turf); one who makes a betting book on sporting events.

Break (to break away, to do a break): To depart in haste.

Breast up to: To accost.

Brisket: The chest.

Brown: A copper coin.

Brums: Tawdry finery (from Brummagem—Birmingham).

Buckley's (Chance): A forlorn hope.

Buck up: Cheer up.

Bump: To meet; to accost aggressively.

Bun, to take the: To take the prize (used ironically).

Bundle, to drop the: To surrender; to give up hope.

Bunk: To sleep in a "bunk" or rough bed. To do a bunk: To depart.

Bunnies, to hawk the: To peddle rabbits.

Bus, to miss the: To neglect opportunities.

Caboose: A small dwelling.

Cat, to whip the: To cry over spilt milk; i.e., to whip the cat that has spilt the milk.

C.B.: Confined to barracks.

Cert: A certainty; a foregone conclusion.

Chap: A "bloke" or "cove".

Chase yourself: Depart; avaunt; "fade away". q.v.

Chat: To address tentatively; to "word", q.v.

Cheque, to pass in one's: To depart this life.

Chew, to chew it over; to chew the rag: To sulk; to nurse a grievance.

Chiack: Vulgar banter; coarse invective.

Chin: To talk; to wag the chin.

Chip: To "chat", q.v. Chip in: To intervene.

Chiv: The face.

Chow: A native of far Cathay.

Chuck up: To relinquish. Chuck off: To chaff; to employ sarcasm.

Chump: A foolish fellow.

Chunk: A lump; a mass.

Clean: Completely; utterly.

Click: A clique; a "push".

Cliner: A young unmarried female.

Clobber: Raiment; vesture.

Cobber: A boon companion.

Collect: To receive one's deserts.

Colour-line: In pugilism, the line drawn by white boxers excluding coloured fighters—for diverse reasons.

Conk: The nose.

Coot: A person of no account (used contemptuously).

Cop: To seize; to secure; also, s., an avocation, a "job".

Cop (or Copper): A police constable.

Copper-top: Red head.

Count, to take the: In pugilism, to remain prostrate for ten counted seconds, and thus lose the fight.

Cove: A "chap" or "bloke". q.v. (Gipsy).

Cow: A thoroughly unworthy, not to say despicable person, place, thing, or circumstance. A fair cow: An utterly obnoxious and otherwise inexpressible person, place, thing or circumstance.

Crack: To smite. s. A blow.

Crack a boo: To divulge a secret; to betray emotion.

Crack hardy: To suppress emotion; to endure patiently; to keep a secret.

Cray: A crayfish.

Crib: A dwelling.

Croak: To die.

Crook: Unwell; dishonest; spurious; fraudulent. Superlative, Dead Crook.

Crool (cruel) the pitch: To frustrate; to interfere with one's schemes or welfare.

Crust: Sustenance; a livelihood.

Cut it out: Omit; discontinue it.

Dago: A native of Southern Europe.

Dash, to do one's: To reach one's Waterloo.

Date: An appointment.

Dawg (dog): A contemptible person; ostentation. To put on dawg: To behave in an arrogant manner.

Dead: In a superlative degree; very.

Deal: To deal it out; to administer punishment; abuse, &c.

Deal: A "hand" at cards.

Deener: A shilling (Fr. Denier. Denarius, a Roman silver coin).

Derry: An aversion; a feud; a dislike.

Dickin: A term signifying distrust or disbelief.

Dile (dial): The face.

Dilly: Foolish; half-witted.

Ding Dong: Strenuous.

Dinkum: Honest; true. "The Dinkum Oil": The truth.

Dipped: Mentally deficient.

Dirt: Opprobrium; a mean speech or action.

Dirty left: A formidable left fist.

Divvies: Dividends; profits.

Dizzy limit: The utmost; the superlative degree.

Do in: To defeat; to kill; to spend.

Done me luck: Lost my good fortune.

Dot in the eye: To strike in the eye.

Douse: To extinguish (Anglo-Saxon).

Drive a quill: To write with a pen; to work in an office.

Duck, to do a: (See "break").

Duds: Personal apparel (Scotch).

Dud: No good; ineffective; used up.

Dutch: German; any native of Central Europe.

'Eads (Heads): The authorities; inner council.

'Eadin': "Heading browns"; tossing pennies.

'Ead over turkey: Heels over head.

'Ead Serang: The chief; the leader.

'Ell fer leather: In extreme haste.

End up, to get: To rise to one's feet.

Fade away, to: To retire; to withdraw.

Fag: A cigarette.

Fair: Extreme; positive.

Fair thing: A wise proceeding; an obvious duty.

Fake: A swindle; a hoax.

Final, to run one's: To die.

Final kick: Final leave.

Finger: An eccentric or amusing person.

Flam: Nonsense; make-believe.

Float, to: To give up the ghost.

Fluff, a bit of: A young female person.

Fly: A turn; a try.

Foot (me foot): A term expressing ridicule.

Frame: The body.

Frill: Affectation.

Furphy: An idle rumour; a canard.

Galoot: A simpleton.

Game: Occupation; scheme; design.

Gawsave: The National Anthem.

Gazob: A fool; a blunderer.

Get, to do a: To retreat hastily.

Gilt: Money; wealth.

Give, to: In one sense, to care.

Gizzard: The heart.

Glarssy: The glassy eye; a glance of cold disdain. The Glassey Alley: The favourite; the most admired.

Glim: A light.
Going (while the going is good): While the path is clear.
Gone (fair gone): Overcome, as with emotion.
Goo-goo eyes: Loving glances.
Gorspil-cove: A minister of the Gospel.
Grandstand play: Playing to the gallery.
Griffin, the straight: The truth; secret information.
Grip: Occupation; employment.
Groggy: Unsteady; dazed.
Grouch: To mope; to grumble.
Grub: Food.
Guff: Nonsense.
Guy: A foolish fellow.
Guy, to do a: To retire.
Guyver: Make-believe.

Handies: A fondling of hands between lovers.
Hang out: To reside; to last.
Hang-over: The aftermath of the night before.
Hitch, to: To wed.
Hitched: Entangled in the bonds of holy matrimony.
Hit things up: To behave strenuously; riotously.
Hokey Fly, by the: A mild expletive, without any particular meaning.
Hot: Excessive; extreme.
Hump, the: A fit of depression.
Hump, to: To carry as a swag or other burden.

Imshee: Begone; retreat; take yourself off.
Intro: Introduction; knock-down. q.v.
It (to be It): To assume a position of supreme importance.

Jane: A woman.
Jiff: A very brief period.
Job, to: To smite.
Joes: Melancholy thoughts.
John: A policeman.
John 'Op (or Jonop): Policeman.
Joint, to jump the: To assume command; to occupy the "joint", i.e., establishment, situation, place of business.
Jolt, to pass a: To deliver a short, sharp blow.
Josser: A simple fellow.
Jug: A prison.

Keep one down: Take a drink.
Keeps, for: For ever; permanently.
Kersplosh: Splash.

Kick: Leave. Kick about: To loaf or hang about.

Kid, to: To deceive; to persuade by flattery.

Kid stakes: Pretence.

King Pin: The leader; the person of chief importance.

Kip: A small chip used for tossing pennies in the occult game of two-up.

Kipsie: A house; the home.

Knob: The head; one in authority.

Knock-down: A ceremony insisted upon by ladies who decline to be "picked up"; a formal introduction.

Knock-out drops: Drugged or impure liquor.

Knock-out punch: A knock-down blow.

Knut: A fop; a well-dressed idler.

Lark: A practical joke; a sportive jest.

Lash: Violence.

Ledding: Leaden.

Leery: Vulgar; low.

Leeuwin: Cape Leeuwin on the South West coast of Australia.

Lid: The hat. To dip the lid: To raise the hat.

Limit: The end; the full length.

Line up; to approach; to accost.

Lingo: Language.

Lip: Impertinence. To give it lip: To talk vociferously.

Little Bourke: Little Bourke Street, Melbourne, Australia.

Little Lons.: Little Lonsdale Street, Melbourne, Australia.

Lob, to: To arrive.

'Loo: Woolloomooloo, a part of Sydney.

Lumme: Love me.

Lurk: A plan of action; a regular occupation.

Mafeesh: Finish; I am finished.

Mag: To scold or talk noisily.

Mallee: A species of Eucalypt; the country where the Mallee grows.

Mash: To woo; to pay court. s. A lover.

Maul: To lay hands upon, either violently or with affection.

Meet, a: An assignation.

Mill: A bout of fisticuffs.

Mix: To mix it; to fight strenuously.

Mizzle: To disappear; to depart suddenly.

Mo.: Abbreviation of "moment".

Moniker: A name; a title; a signature.

Mooch: To saunter about aimlessly.

Moon: To loiter.

Mud, my name is: i.e., I am utterly discredited.

Mug: A fool; also the mouth.

Mug, to: To kiss.

Mug: A simpleton.

Mullock, to poke: To deride; to tease.

Mushy: Sentimental.

Nail: Catch.

Nark: s. A spoil-sport; a churlish fellow.

Nark, to: To annoy; to foil.

Natchril: Natural.

Neck and neck: Side by side.

Neck, to get it in the: To receive severe punishment, i.e., "Where the chicken got the axe."

Nick: Physical condition; good health.

Nipper: A small boy.

Nix: Nothing.

Nod, on the: Without payment.

Nose around, to: To seek out inquisitively.

Nothing (ironically): Literally "something considerable".

Odds, above the: Beyond the average; outside the pale.

Oopizootics: An undiagnosed complaint.

Orfis (office): A warning; a word of advice; a hint.

Oricle (oracle), to work the: To secure desired results.

Orl (orl in): Without limit or restriction.

'Ot Socks: Gaily coloured hose.

Out, to: To render unconscious with a blow.

Out, all: Quite exhausted; fully extended.

Pack, to send to the: To relegate to obscurity.

Pal: A friend; a mate (Gipsy).

Pard: A partner; a mate.

Part: Give; hand over.

Pass (pass 'im one): To deliver a blow.

Pat, on one's: Alone; single-handed.

Peach: A desirable young woman; "fresh as a peach".

Peb (pebble): A flash fellow; a "larrikin".

Phiz: The face.

Pick at: To chaff; to annoy.

Pick up, to: To dispense with the ceremony of a "knock-down" or introduction.

Pilot cove: A clergyman.

Pile it on: To rant; to exaggerate.

Pinch: To steal; to place under arrest.

Pins: Legs.

227

Pip: A fit of depression.

Pitch a tale: To trump up an excuse; to weave a romance.

Plant: To bury.

Plug: To smite with the fist.

Plug along, to: To proceed doggedly.

Plunk: An exclamation expressing the impact of a blow.

Podgy: Fat; plump.

Point: The region of the jaw; much sought after by pugilists.

Point, to: To seize unfair advantage; to scheme.

Pole, up the: Distraught through anger, fear, &c.; also, disappeared, vanished.

Pot, a: A considerable amount; as a "pot of money".

Pot, the old: The male parent (from "Rhyming Slang", the "old pot and pan"—"old man").

Prad: A horse.

Pug: A pugilist.

Pull my (or your) leg: To deceive or get the best of.

Pull, off: Desist.

Pull, to take a: To desist; to discontinue.

Punch a cow: To conduct a team of oxen.

Punter: The natural prey of a "bookie". q.v.

Push: A company of rowdy fellows gathered together for ungentle purposes.

Push up the daisies, to: To be interred.

Queer the pitch: To frustrate; to fool.

Quid: A sovereign, or pound sterling.

Quod: Prison.

Rabbit, to run the: To convey liquor from a public-house.

Rag, to chew the: To grieve; to brood.

Rag, to sky the: To throw a towel into the air in token of surrender (pugilism).

Rain, to keep out the: To avoid danger; to act with caution.

Rat: A street urchin; a wharf loafer.

Rattled: Excited; confused.

Recomember: Remember.

Red 'ot: Extreme; out-and-out.

Registry: The office of a Registrar.

Renege: To fail to follow suit (in playing cards); to quit.

Ribuck: Correct, genuine; an interjection signifying assent

Rile: To annoy. Riled: Roused to anger.

Ring, the: The arena of a prize-fight.

Ring, the dead: A remarkable likeness.

Ringer: Expert.

Rise, a: An accession of fortune; an improvement.

Rocks: A locality in Sydney.

Rook, to: To "take down".

Rorty: Boisterous; rowdy.

Roust, or rouse: To upbraid with many words.

'Roy: Fitzroy, a suburb of Melbourne; its football team.

Ructions: Growling; argument.

Run against: To meet more or less unexpectedly.

Run 'is final: Died.

Saints: A football team of St Kilda, Victoria.

Sandy blight: Ophthalmia.

Savvy: Commonsense; shrewdness.

Sawing wood: "Bluffing"; biding one's time.

School: A club; a clique of gamblers, or others.

Scoot: To hurry; to scuttle.

Scran: Food.

Scrap: Fight.

Set, to: To attack; to regard with disfavour.

Set, to have: To have marked down for punishment or revenge.

Shick, shickered: Intoxicated.

Shook: Stolen; disturbed.

Shook on: Infatuated.

Shyin', or Shine: Excellent; desirable.

Sight: To tolerate; to permit; also to see; observe.

Sir Garneo: In perfect order; satisfactory.

Skirt, or bit of skirt: A female.

Skite: To boast. Skiter: A boaster.

Sky the wipe: See "Rag".

Slab: A portion; a tall, awkward fellow.

Slam: Making all the tricks (in card-playing).

Slanter: Spurious; unfair.

Slap-up: Admirable; excellent.

Slats: The ribs.

Slick: Smart; deft; quick.

Sling: Discard; throw.

Slope, to: To elope; to leave in haste.

Sloppy: Lachrymose; maudlin.

Slushy: A toiler in a scullery.

Smoodge: To flatter or fawn; to bill and coo.

Smoodger: A sycophant; a courtier.

Snag: A hindrance; formidable opponent.

Snake-'eaded: Annoyed, vindictive.

229

Snake juice: Strong drink.

Snare: To acquire; to seize; to win.

Snarkey: Angry.

Snide: Inferior; or no account.

Snob: A bootmaker.

Snort: To bear a grudge.

Snouted: Treated with disfavour.

Snuff, or snuff it: To expire.

Sock it into: To administer physical punishment.

Solid: Severe; severely.

So-long: A form of farewell.

Sool: To attack; to urge on.

Soot, leadin': A chief attribute.

Sore, to get: To become aggrieved.

Sore-head: A curmudgeon.

Sour, to turn, or get: To become pessimistic or discontented.

Spank: To chastise maternal-wise.

Spar: A gentle bout at fisticuffs.

Spare me days: A pious ejaculation.

Specs.: Spectacles.

Splash: To expend.

Splice: To join in matrimony.

Spout: To preach or speak at length.

Sprag: To accost truculently.

Spruik: To deliver a speech, as a showman.

Spuds: Potatoes.

Square: Upright, honest.

Square an' all: Of a truth; verily.

Squeak: To give away a secret.

Squiz: A brief glance.

Stand-orf: Retiring; reticent.

Stajum: Stadium, where prize-fights are conducted.

Stiffened: Bought over.

Stiff-un: A corpse.

Stoke: To nourish; to eat.

Stop a pot: To quaff ale.

Stop one: To receive a blow.

Straight, on the: In fair and honest fashion.

Strength of it: The truth of it; the value of it.

Stretch, to do a: To serve a term of imprisonment.

Strike: The innocuous remnant of a hardy curse.

Strike: To discover; to meet.

Strike me!: The innocuous remnant of a hard curse.

Strong, going: Proceeding with vigour.

'Struth: An emaciated oath.

Stuff: Money.

Stunt: A performance; a tale.

Swad, Swaddy: A private soldier.

Swank: Affectation; ostentation.

Swap: To exchange.

Swell: An exalted person.

Swig: A draught of water or other liquid.

Swiv'ly: Afraid, or unable, to look straight.

Tabbie: A female.

Take down: Deceive; get the best of.

Take 'em on: Engage them in battle.

Take it out: To undergo imprisonment in lieu of a fine.

Tart: A young woman (contraction of sweetheart).

Tater: Potato.

Tenner: A ten-pound note.

Throw in the alley: To surrender.

Time, to do: To serve a term in prison.

Time, to have no time for: To regard with impatient disfavour.

Tip: To forecast; to give; to warn.

Tipple: Strong drink; to indulge in strong drink.

Toff: An exalted person.

Togs: Clothes.

Togged: Garbed.

Tom: A girl.

Tony: Stylish.

Took: Arrested; apprehended.

Top, off one's: Out of one's mind.

Top off, to: To knock down; to assault.

Toss in the towel: See "rag".

Tossed out on my neck: Rejected.

Touch: Manner; mode; fashion.

Tough: Unfortunate; hardy; also a "tug". q.v.

Tough luck: Misfortune.

Track with: To woo; to "go walking with".

Treat, a: Excessively; abundantly.

Tucked away: Interred.

Tucker: Food.

Tug: An uncouth fellow; a hardy rogue.

Tumble to, or to take a tumble: To comprehend suddenly.

Turkey, head over: Heels over head.

Turn down: To reject; to dismiss.

Turn, out of one's: Impertinently; uninvited.
Twig: To observe; to espy.

Umpty: An indefinite numeral.
Umptydoo: Far-fetched; "crook".
Upper-cut: In pugilism, an upward blow.
Uppish: Proud.
Up to us: Our turn; our duty.

Vag, on the: Under the provisions of the Vagrancy Act.

Wade in: Take your fill.
Wallop: To beat, chastise.
Waster: A reprobate; an utterly useless and unworthy person.
Waterworks, turn on the: To shed tears.
Welt: A blow.
Wet, to get: To become incensed; ill-tempered.
Whips: Abundance.
White (white man): A true, sterling fellow.
White-headed boy: A favourite; a pet.
Willin': Strenuous; hearty.
Win, a: Success.
Wise, to get: To comprehend; to unmask deceit.
Wise, to put: To explain; to instruct.
Wolf: To eat.
Word: To accost with fair speech.
Wot price: Behold; how now!
Wowser: A narrow-minded, intolerant person.

Yakker: Hard toil.
Yap: To talk volubly.
Yowling: Wailing; caterwauling.